What Does the Bible Say About That?

A Biblical Worldview Curriculum for Children

What Does the Bible Say About That?

A Biblical Worldview Curriculum for Children

Kevin Swanson

Generations
PASSING ON THE FAITH

ISBN: 978-0-9833505-6-9

Cover art by Daniel Nuckols
Cover design by Rei Suzuki and Winslow Robbins
Illustrations by Tammy Sechrist
Typeset and Layout by David Sechrist

Published by:
Generations
19039 Plaza Dr. Ste. 210
Parker, Colorado 80134
www.generations.org

For more information on this and
other titles from Generations,
visit www.generations.org or call 888-389-9080.

Contents

A Message to Parents (Teachers)

If education is a building, some books will give you beautiful wall murals for decor, some will give you the window sills, some will give you the doors, and some will give you the wood framing. What you hold in your hands is concrete for the foundations. It is important that an education have good, solid concrete footers upon which the system of knowledge will rest. That is the purpose of this manual. We present the basic concrete footers of a Christian worldview in language that a child can understand.

Over the last 25 years, the Nehemiah Institute has conducted its "PEERS Worldview Test" for Christian children in homeschools, Christian schools, and public schools. Based on a study of 60,000 students, the survey found that Christians attending public schools slipped 86% (from a score of 38.9 to 5.4) over 21 years. Christian children attending traditional Christian schools slipped 65% over 21 years (from a score of 49.7 to 17.3), and homeschoolers and Christian schoolers that were taught the rudiments of a biblical worldview actually improved by 11% (from 62.1 to 69.4) over the same period. The baseline scoring was established by testing self-proclaimed atheists and humanists (against Christian pastors and leaders who held to the inerrancy and authority of the Bible). According to these studies, a score of 38 would indicate a "secular humanist." Thus, you can see that most Christian children have become secular humanists if they attended Christian schools or public schools. [1]

Ideas matter. What you teach your children really matters. Your choice of curriculum is vitally important. Because of the secular humanism taught in schools and textbooks everywhere, some families will see their children leave the faith in this generation. Some families will see their grandchildren leave the Christian faith. Actually, the entire English-speaking world is in the process of abandoning the Christian faith. This has already worked terrible effects on the family and the socio-economic conditions in western nations. But more important than all of that is your children's relationship with the true and living God. When God is ignored, and His truth is put on the back burner, children wander away from Him. They forget about Him, because they do not rest their system of knowledge on His truth.

Of course, all parents that love their children will seek the best possible education and training for them. We want to see our children in heaven someday. Therefore, what they believe about God, about His creation, about truth, sin, and redemption really matters.

Speaking of the man who hears God's words and does them, Jesus said, "The wise man built his house upon the rock." This strong foundation is God's truth revealed to us in the Bible. When a nation builds its system of knowledge and its education on the wrong foundations, it sets the nation on footers of sand. Its buildings and institutions may not come down right away, but one day the rains will come and floods will rise, and "great will be the fall of that house!" (Matthew 7:27) Then our nation will see 42% of its children born without fathers (up from 6% in 1960). Its scientific technology and genetic engineering will become self-destructive. Birth implosions and the breakdown of character will turn its economies upside down. Our nation might even turn into the greatest debtor nation in the world.

It is time right now to teach your children the basics. Give them a biblical worldview, and they will have what it takes to withstand the storms to come.

---

[1] www. nehemiahinstitute.com

How to Use This Manual

There are ten lessons, each of which includes text, memory verses, and follow-up activities. Most children should be able to finish the book in about ten weeks of regular study. An answer key is provided at the end of the manual, which you may remove if you wish.

This curriculum was designed to fulfill one half of a year of the social studies requirement for 5th to 7th grade.

Our hope is that this curriculum will work as a self-study course for the average student. Your student may need a little help with some of the vocabulary. Serious effort was employed to keep the language simple and straightforward and to explain the more difficult concepts in language a child would understand. It may be wise to have the student finish the vocabulary exercise in each lesson before reading the text.

1 The First Thing You Need to Know

Proverbs 1:7

The fear of the LORD is the beginning of knowledge: but fools despise wisdom and instruction.

The First Thing You Need to Know

What do you know? Surely, you have learned many things up to this point in your life. Try to think of several things that you have learned. Now, how do you know that these things you have learned are really true? Maybe you trust people when they tell you the moon is made out of cheese. Maybe you have looked at the sky with your eyes and decided that the sky was blue. Well, maybe your eyes are fooling you. How do you know that the things you have learned are true and right? We will answer this question in this chapter.

But before we answer this question, there is one very important thing you need to know. It comes from God's book of wisdom — the Book of Proverbs. It is the very first lesson in this important book. It is the most basic lesson of all.

The fear of the LORD is the beginning of knowledge: but fools despise wisdom and instruction.

Proverbs 1:7

Before we speak of the most important truths you will ever learn, it is very important that you fear God. If you do not believe in God and reverence God, you will probably fall for lies, because there are so many lies in the world. Fearing God is the very beginning of wisdom. If your parents fear God, and if you fear God, you are starting in a very safe place. You have a good foundation for knowing the truth.

Watch Out for Liars!

There are people who lie, and there are people who tell the truth. There are books that lie to you, and there are books that tell you the truth. So you must be careful with what you read and what you hear.

There are different kinds of lies. Of course, it is always wrong to lie, but some people tell very big lies, and some people tell smaller, less significant lies.

From Psalm 14 we learn that it takes a fool to tell a very big lie. Here is a very big lie. In fact, his may be the biggest lie of all: "There is no God." As you grow older, you need to keep an eye and an ear out for people who tell lies. You must be careful not to believe everything that you hear. If one person says there is a God, and another person says there is no God, they cannot both be right. How do you know who is right in these arguments? This study guide will introduce you to several very important matters about things like truth, right and wrong, government, family, and church. As you grow older, you will learn more about these things. But for now, you need to learn the basics about the most important things in life.

What Is True?

We begin with this simple question: "What is true?" This is a very important question. What would happen if you believed a lie? Suppose your friend told you that the ice on a lake was very thick, and you could walk across the lake without any problems. What if it turned out that your friend told you a lie, and the ice was only about one inch thick towards the middle of the lake? Wouldn't you have liked to know the truth before you walked across the lake? It would be very dangerous if you believed that lie because you might fall through the ice and drown in the lake.

The truth is important. But whom should we believe? Many people in this world tell lies. Some do not know they are telling lies. There are lots of lies everywhere. So whom do we believe?

There is only one good answer to that question. We cannot trust in men, but we can always trust in God. We must believe that there is a God before we can talk about anything else. God is our source of truth, so if there is no God, then we have no sure truth. We still have a lot of ignorant men who tell lies and contradict each other. Do you see how important it is to believe in God?

And the LORD God formed man of the dust of the ground, and breathed into his nostrils the breath of life; and man became a living being.

Genesis 2:7

God Gives Man Truth

God created us and everything else, and He talks to us so we know that He made us. This happened with Adam at the very beginning of the world. When Adam woke up and looked around him, how did he know that there was a God? How did he know that he had a relationship with God? Of course, it was because God spoke to him and gave him a few instructions. "Hey Adam, you can eat of all the trees of this garden, except for one," He said. "Cultivate the garden and take good care of it." We find these first words from God in Genesis 2.

And the LORD God commanded the man, saying, "Of every tree of the garden you may freely eat; but of the tree of the knowledge of good and evil you shall not eat, for in the day that you eat of it you shall surely die."

Genesis 2:16-17

Here we are many years later, and we still need God's Word. Adam needed to hear from God in the garden. But now, even after sin and evil things came into the world (like sickness and death), we still need God to talk to us. We also need to listen to Him because He is still the One who gives us truth.

Thankfully, over about four thousand years, God talked to His people. There were men who wrote down some of the things God said. We know that God spoke to Adam, Noah, Abraham, Moses, David, John the Baptist, and Jesus' disciples. These writings were collected and put into a book that we call "The Holy Bible."

All Scripture is given by inspiration of God, and is profitable for doctrine, for reproof, for correction, for instruction in righteousness, that the man of God may be complete, thoroughly equipped for every good work.

2 Timothy 3:16-17

Some people ignore the Bible and say that God speaks directly to them instead. This is dangerous. Remember that everybody has his own opinion, and sometimes people like to pretend that they received their ideas from something God said to them privately. But these are just more opinions from man. Often, they are just more lies in this world of millions of lies. If we want to find the truth, we must go to the collection of God's words that have stood the test of time.

The Book That Always Tells the Truth

The Bible is the book that always tells the truth. We may not all agree on what the Bible means to say about some things. But when it comes to questions of truth, our discussions must center around the Bible. We need to go back to the Bible again and again in our search for truth.

Many Christians treat the Bible as a book they use to worship God on Sundays, but they don't use it on Monday, Tuesday, or the rest of the days of the week. They don't use it to guide their family life. They don't use it to decide who to vote for in the government. So the Bible is useless to them.

You just read 2 Timothy 3:16-17. In these verses, Paul is talking about how the Old and New Testament were given to prepare the man of God for every good work. It is trustworthy. It speaks with authority and is a very useful book!

A Biblical Worldview

In this study guide we are explaining the basics of what we call a "Biblical World-view." Now that's a big word! It is an important word that you should understand. Having a worldview is like looking at the world through colored glasses.
If you looked at the room around you while wearing pink glasses, everything would appear pink. The couch would look pink, the chairs would also look pink. Even the

green grass outside would look pink to you. Well, everybody sees the world and understands the world through these worldview glasses. Some people's glasses are green, so they see the world as green. Some people's glasses are pink, so they see the world as pink. Some people's glasses are blue, and they would see the world as blue. Can you see how a person's worldview colors what he sees? But many people are wearing the wrong glasses, so they see the world incorrectly. It is important that you have the right pair of glasses on so that you see the world as it really is.

The Bible gives us the best glasses through which to see the world. It provides us with the biblical worldview. But how can you know if somebody has a "Biblical Worldview"? Here is a simple test: ask him about anything. Ask him about something related to food, or love, or dads and moms, or government, or music. If this fellow has a biblical worldview, in some way or another he will always bring up the question, "WHAT DOES THE BIBLE SAY ABOUT THAT?" He will always start with the Bible, before he thinks about anything else.

Other Worldviews

As you grow up, you will learn that not everyone agrees on these things. Many wear the wrong kind of glasses as they look at the world around them. Sadly, there are people in the world who do not agree with God. They do not think His Word is truth. They want to trust their own opinions rather than rely on their Creator to teach them what is true.

But we are not going to look at other worldviews in this study. When you get older, you will learn about these other worldviews and all of the lies that they tell. When people believe other worldviews, they do not learn the beginning of true knowledge, which is the fear of the Lord (Proverbs 1:7). If they believe these false worldviews, they trust in a lie. Remember the story of the lie about the ice on the lake? If you trust in a lie, you might just fall through the ice and drown. But what happens to people who believe in the wrong worldview?

The Bible tells us that those who trust in a lying worldview "will have their place in the lake which burns with fire and brimstone" (Revelation 21:8). So you can see that these are very serious matters.

What About Smart Scientists?

Nowadays, we have smart scientists who tell us that the first man came from an ape through a process called evolution. These men will tell you that your great-great-great-great grandfather (long ago) was an animal like an ape. Now, if you have a Biblical worldview, you need to ask the question. Do you remember the question? Here's a hint: W.D.T.B.S.A.T.? Here is a verse from the Bible about the creation of the man:

"And the Lord God formed man of the dust of the ground, and breathed into his nostrils the breath of life."

Genesis 2:7

On the one hand, some scientists tell you that man came from monkeys over millions of years, but God says that He created man out of the dust while he was creating the world in six days. Who are you going to believe — God or the scientist?

Scientists believe they have "evidence," and they are confident that they are very smart. Most of the time these scientists do not believe they can make a mistake when they study their "evidence" about apes turning into men. But is it possible that they have made some mistakes? Actually, there are many scientists who disagree with the scientists that think man came from an ape over millions of years.

So it is always safe to start with what God says. We should be careful about looking at dead fossils in the rocks and making big, brave claims about what happened over millions of years. There is only one safe way to find out what happened at the creation of the world. Ask somebody who was there. Were you there? Was the scientist there? Who was there at the beginning of the world? Of course, God was there.

Maybe we should ask Him.

For in six days the LORD made the heavens and the earth, the sea, and all that is in them, and rested the seventh day. Therefore the LORD blessed the Sabbath day and hallowed it.

Exodus 20:11

Chapter 1 Review

Scripture Memory

Proverbs 1:7

The fear of the LORD is the beginning of knowledge: but fools despise wisdom and instruction.

Scripture Reading

Romans 3:3-4

For what if some did not believe? Will their unbelief make the faithfulness of God without effect? Certainly not! Indeed, let God be true but every man a liar. As it is written: "That You may be justified in Your words, and may overcome when You are judged."

Proverbs 9:10

The fear of the LORD is the beginning of wisdom, and the knowledge of the Holy One is understanding.

Psalm 14

The fool has said in his heart, "There is no God." They are corrupt, they have done abominable works, there is none who does good. The LORD looks down from heaven upon the children of men, to see if there are any who understand, who seek God. They have all turned aside, they have together become corrupt, there is none who does good, no, not one. Have all the workers of iniquity no knowledge, who eat up my people as they eat bread, and do not call on the LORD? There they are in great fear, for God is with the generation of the righteous. You shame the counsel of the poor, but the LORD is his refuge. Oh, that the salvation of Israel would come out of Zion! When the LORD brings back the captivity of His people, let Jacob rejoice and Israel be glad.

1. What is the biggest lie that people tell? (Hint: See Psalm 14:1.)

_____

_____

2. What is the beginning of wisdom and knowledge?

_____

_____

3. What might happen to you if you believed a lie (such as your friend telling you that the ice in the lake could hold you when it was only one inch thick)?

_____

_____

_____

4. Why can you trust in God completely, while at the same time you cannot trust in men completely?

_____

_____

_____

5. What did God create?

_____

6. What did God say to Adam as soon as He created him? (Hint: See Genesis 2)

_____

_____

7. Why is it even more important for us to get revelation from God after the fall?

_____

_____

_____

8. Where can we find God's truth?

_____

9. Give examples of men who God spoke to in the Old Testament and the New Testament.

_____

_____

10. What is the use of the Bible (according to 2 Timothy 3:16-17)?

_____

_____

11. Many Christians use the Bible to worship God on Sunday. Can we use the Bible for anything else? Give some other examples.

_____

_____

_____

12. Why is the Bible trustworthy?

_____

_____

13. What is a good way to remember what a worldview is?

_____

14. How would you know if somebody had a biblical world-view?

_____

_____

_____

 15. According to Revelation 21:8, what happens to people who believe and trust in a lie?

_____

_____

16. What does W.D.T.B.S.A.T. stand for?

_____

_____

17. If God's Word disagrees with scientists, who are you going to believe?

_____

18. If a scientist found a dead animal in a rock, and he told you that it was 50 million years old, what would you ask him?
W_____ Y_____ T_____?

19. How did God create man (according to Genesis 2)?

_____

_____

_____

Vocabulary

Match the word with the correct definition on the right-hand side of the page.

Words	Definitions
Truth	A direction or order
Significant	Able or likely to cause harm or injury
Dangerous	The power or right to give orders, make decisions, and enforce obedience
Ignorant	That which is true or in accordance with fact or reality
Relationship	Important
Instructions	A particular philosophy of life or conception of the world
Cultivate	Stupid or uninformed
Opinion	Able to be relied on as honest or truthful
Authority	Feeling or showing certainty about something
Trustworthy	The way in which two people are connected
Worldview	A view or judgment formed about something, not necessarily based on fact or knowledge
Confident	Prepare or use land for sowing or planting
Fossils	The remains or impression of a creature preserved in petrified form or as a mold or cast in rock

Word Search!

```
R B W E G L A S S E S N D Y S E O A
G L E B G B X S X J F G Y T C P S P
W D G L I D U D Z V R T N I I O T Y
E C Y B I G E T B E P V X R E S U E
F X L G Z E R L H X R Y W O N L M H
N E T D U U V Q W O Q B R H T F R O
P G F E Q L F E T O D V L T I V S B
H E H N I U Q I P I N C W U S V M J
D B Y X C L Z I W J J K J A T A Y S
F F O M G C X O Q N J I D X S T U H
I E V I V W R D E G J T H V T H I D
B L I N R L E Q I K W U U M R P A A
D S N B D P P S U X H H H W U D L U
Z K D V P F Q Z E F V I U R T O P V
A A I I F G N I N N I G E B H G H S
T E U E Y S H J L D G T O E K B V T
W Q I B V P J M V R Z J M A D A F V
E A Z L G B G R L F A W R T U T C Q
```

Find each of these words in the box above. Circle them when you find them. They may be horizontal, vertical, or diagonal.

Worldview	Glasses	Scientists
Beginning	Adam	Believe
Truth	Bible	God
Lie	Authority	
Knowledge	Equipped	

Chapter 2

The World Around You: Where Did Everything Come From?

Genesis 1:1

In the beginning God created the heavens and the earth.

The World Around You:
Where Did Everything Come From?

Look around you. What do you see? Perhaps you can see grass, trees, houses, chairs, sofas, dogs, and cats. Do you know where all of this came from? You know there had to be somebody who made the furniture and the houses. They didn't just appear out of nowhere. Men take trees and rocks and turn them into furniture and houses. But who made the trees and the rocks? Who made men with the brains to make the houses and cars?

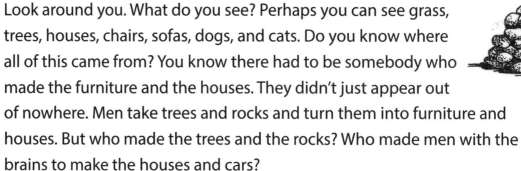

People disagree about the origin of all these things. Almost everyone would agree that people make cars and houses out of material like trees and rocks. But where do trees and rocks come from? There is a lot of disagreement on this, but there are only three possible explanations:

1. Nothing made the trees and people, because they have always existed.
2. The trees and people came about by accident in a chance universe.
3. Someone made the trees and people.

Only one of these explanations really tells how everything came into existence. Most people who have been educated in universities teach the second theory. These smart people believe that trees, rocks, cats, dogs, and even people evolved by accident in a chance universe. Of course, nobody has ever seen this happen.

26

They don't know HOW it could happen. But there are people who believe that is the way everything came into existence. What would happen if you put a firecracker in a bowl of sand and watched it blow up? Do you think that the sand would turn into a sand castle? Or would the sand turn into a jumping frog? This would be very hard to imagine. There would be no scientific explanation for something like that happening. But many smart people believe that is how trees and people came to be. These people say that everything came into existence by "chance."

How did these trees, rocks, and people come into this world? Christians answer this very big question with two words — "creation" and "providence."

Westminster Shorter Catechism
Questions 9 & 11

Question 9: What is the work of creation?
The work of creation is, God's making all things of nothing, by the word of His power, in the space of six days, and all very good.

Question 11: What are God's works of providence?
God's works of providence are, His most holy, wise, and powerful preserving and governing all His creatures, and all their actions.

Creation

Many worldly philosophers and scientists sit and wonder about basic questions. They ask, "Where did I come from? Am I real?" They cannot answer the most basic questions of life. They don't know where they came from, and they don't know who they are! Isn't that sad? They wonder about these things because they do not want to believe in God or in God's revelation (the Bible). Thankfully, the Bible does not leave us wondering about how all of this came about. The very first verse of the Bible gives us the most basic clue concerning where we came from.

In the beginning, God created the heavens and the earth.

Genesis 1:1

All of the material things that you see in the universe were created by God in the beginning. Of course, there is a re-shaping and re-forming of things going on all the time. Suppose that your father gave you one pound of clay, and you made many fine little creations out of the clay. You make little houses, birds, cows, and hats out of the clay. But you still have the same clay. In many ways this is what God provides in the universe. At the beginning He provided the materials for the heavens and the earth. Then, He created the first plants and animals and the first human beings. This all happened during the six days of creation. Out of these first plants and animals came other plants and animals. From the first human beings (Adam and Eve) came many other human beings.

For in six days the LORD made the heavens and the earth, the sea, and all that is in them, and rested the seventh day.

Exodus 20:11

Providence

Not all of the rocks we see now appeared when God created the heavens and the earth. Many were formed later on through various events. Now some people believe that the rocks and the mountains were formed by chance events. They say that over a long period of time many volcanoes and big floods formed the rocks that sit on the surface of the earth today. But we know that many of the rocks and mountains formed because of volcanoes and a big flood. In fact, we have record in the Bible that there was a very large worldwide flood that formed much of the continents and the entire surface of the earth. But did this flood come about by accident? What about the thousands of earthquakes, volcanoes, and floods that have happened all around the globe over thousands of years? For example, a volcano called Mount St. Helens made some very large rocks and very deep canyons in 1980. Did all of these natural disasters, including Noah's big flood, happen by accident? Not at all!

When Noah's large flood came and covered the earth, God meant it to happen.

For after seven more days I will cause it to rain on the earth forty days and forty nights, and I will destroy from the face of the earth all living things that I have made.

Genesis 7:4

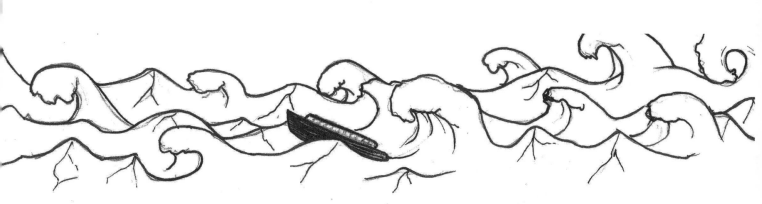

From Genesis 7:4 we learn that God meant to kill the plants, the animals, and the people on the earth. God brought this flood to our world because He wanted to do it. He brought it because men had become very wicked. Many people died in that flood, and they died because God brought that flood to destroy them. Many people today find this very upsetting. But we need to remember that God cares about His earth, and He is watching the men who persist in doing evil things. He is involved, and He brings a judgment on them when He chooses.

Although you cannot see God, you must know that He is involved in His world. He purposes everything that happens, and nothing happens outside of His control. Look around the room right now. Look at the people, the chairs, the furniture, and the little dust particles falling through the air. God has put this moment together. It was God who appointed every one of your family members to be born and to be here right now. It was God who provided this little house where your family could live together. It was God who made sure that this would be a cold day or a hot day. Every part of your reality is put together by God Himself!

What Is Real?

Some things are real, but some things are merely pretend and imaginary. For example, a writer named J.R.R. Tolkien came up with a funny little hairy-toed creature called a "hobbit." These hobbit creatures are supposed to be something like little men with hairy toes who eat three breakfasts, two lunches, and several dinners each day. Of course, these hobbits don't really exist. They are only pretend creatures.

But how do you know that hobbits are pretend? Have you ever seen a hobbit? How do you know that dogs are real? Have you ever seen a dog? This is one way we confirm that something is real. If we can see it, then it may be real.

There are people who do not believe that God is real. They tell us that God is not real because they have not seen God. Have you ever seen God? Of course, you have seen trees and dogs and human beings, but have you ever seen God?

There are some things that we believe are real that we have never seen. We speak of "love." But have you ever seen "love"? Perhaps you have seen your father act lovingly towards your mother. But have you ever seen "love"? Have you ever bumped into "love" like you might bump into a tree? Of course not! So just because you cannot see God does not mean He doesn't exist. The Bible tells us that God is a Spirit (John 4:24). So of course you cannot see God.

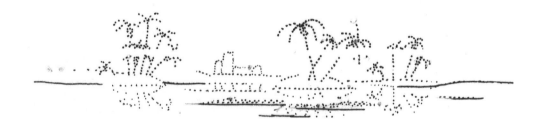

Should You Always Believe Your Eyes?

Have you ever seen a mirage in the desert? It looks like a pool of water, but when you come closer to it, you find nothing but more desert sand. Sometimes your eyes fool you. But if you cannot believe your eyes, what can you believe? You should remember from the last chapter what the most reliable source of truth is. What is the book that never lies? Of course, it is the Holy Bible. This book never lies because it is the Word of God. So to find out what is real, you must go to the Bible where you can learn about God's world and God's reality. From the first chapter in the Bible, we find out right away some things that are real: God, Light, Man, Plants, Birds.

To find out what is real, you must go to the Bible where you can learn about God's world and God's reality.

From the very first chapter in the Bible, we learn about the things that are real. We learn that God is real. Light is real. So are plants, birds, animals, and man. If God says these things are real, then we believe that they are real. Even if you are blind and you never get to see a bird, you can believe that birds are real because God's Word tells you that they are real! We also believe that God is real because the Bible tells us that He is real.

The Most Difficult Question in the World

There are some things in our world that are very hard to understand. Many proud smart guys who teach in colleges do not like to admit this. Proud men want to think that they know everything. That's what makes them so proud!

But Christians admit right away that they don't understand everything. In fact, they don't even understand the most basic things about reality. Actually, the smartest men in the world cannot answer the most basic questions about the world, either. Here, are some of the questions they cannot answer:

How did this world come about?

How did something appear out of nothing?

How does God create the world out of nothing?

How did God create one piece of dirt out of nothing?

What are the most basic building blocks of matter?

What are the protons and neutrons in an atom made out of?

What is light?

These are very basic questions, but the smartest men cannot answer them! Now there is one more question that is the most difficult question of all. The smartest men in the world have never answered it. Here is the question:

Is the world made out of one thing, or is it made out of many things?

Let me try to explain the problem. If reality is one, then there cannot be change and we cannot say that one thing is separate or different from something else. If everything is one big blob, then I am not a different person from you, for example. On the other hand, if reality is many things, then there can be no order in the world. We would never be able to organize things. We could never organize our ideas. We could never organize our socks in one drawer, our shirts in another drawer, and our pants in another drawer. We would live in a very disorganized world! If we could not organize our ideas, we would never be able to develop language. We would not be able to think, or speak to each other! If you cannot understand this very well, that's alright. Don't worry about it! It is a very difficult question, and even the great philosophers, the smartest men in the world have never figured this one out.

The Bible Answers the Most Difficult Question in the World

But now we need to ask the question: "What does the Bible say about that? As it turns out, the Bible has the answer to the most difficult question in the world. Smart men in big colleges that don't believe the Bible cannot answer this question. Smart philosophers have never answered the question. But here is how the Bible answers the question:

God is One, and God is Three Persons

Of all the things that are real, God is the ultimate reality, the highest reality. You cannot find anything more ultimate than God. **And, God is One, and God is Three Persons.**

I told you that you would not be able to understand it completely. Think about it this way. Scientists have studied the human body and counselors have studied the human soul for thousands of years. They have written many books on the human body. They still don't understand human beings entirely. If we cannot fully understand human beings, does it make sense that we cannot understand God either? God is more complicated than you and I. God is beyond our comprehension! Even if we were to write 10,000 books about God, we would never fully understand Him. We can know a little bit about Him, because He tells us about Himself. But we can never know everything about Him.

What we do know from the Bible is that there is only One God. "Hear, O Israel, the Lord our God is one Lord" (Deut. 6:4).

We also know that Jesus is God (John 1:1). He made the universe (John 1:3), and He saves His people from their sins (Matt. 1:21). Only God can provide salvation (Job 40:14). We also know that the Father is God (Eph. 1:3, 1 Pet. 1:3, Col. 1:3). We also know that the Spirit is God (Eph. 4:30).

Finally, we know that the Father, the Son, and the Spirit talk to each other and love each other. We call this persons in relationship with each other.

Now, how can all three distinct persons each be fully God and there still be One God? This question will blow your mind! We cannot fully understand this. But this idea that God is One and Three is still very important. It is important for every part of your life. Think about these questions for a moment:

Should your house be completely organized and clean all the time? Or should you allow for a little disorder while you're getting things done?

Should human beings be rounded up into big government programs that maintain total control and total unity? Or should there be no government at all and should people be allowed to do whatever they want to do?

Should you learn about many things in your education? Or should you learn about one thing?

Should our art be boring by focusing on unity? Or should our art be chaotic, disorganized, and disconnected?

The Problem with No Unity

If there is no unity in the world, then everything is disorganized and chaotic. In civil society, people would run around stealing each other's money and killing each other. There would be no relationships, no family, and no churches. It would be anarchy.

The Problem with Absolute Unity

If there was absolute unity in the world, then everything would be boring. Big governments turn into frightening tyrannies. There would not be any freedom for the individuals and families in the society.

When countries turn away from the Bible and the God of the Bible, they will become more chaotic OR more tyrannical. They will fail to achieve the balance of Unity and Diversity. It is only when we believe in the God of the Bible, and follow His words (or laws) in the Bible, that we will get a good balance in our countries.

God Is Sovereign

When we say that God is sovereign, we mean that He is in control over everything that happens. Have you ever seen a little bird lying on the ground, wounded or dead? Do you think that God knows about that little bird? Of course He does. There may be 253,000 birds that are falling to the ground around the world right now. God knows about every single one of them. They get hurt and die, according to His plan and purpose. And, of course, He makes sure that more mama birds are having babies to replace the ones that have died.

> Are not two sparrows sold for a copper coin? And not one of them falls to the ground apart from your Father's will.
>
> **Matthew 10:29**

Find a pair of dice. Before you throw the dice, decide on what numbers you would like to roll. Will you roll double 1s or double 6s? Throw the dice and see if you can get what you planned to roll. God knew what you would roll before you rolled the dice. He knew it because He determined it. Of course, you did not have the power to make sure that you rolled what you planned to roll. But God has determined what everyone who is playing with dice will roll today, tomorrow, and every other day. He has determined everything that happens and will happen.

> The lot is cast into the lap, but its every decision is from the LORD.
>
> **Proverbs 16:33**

Man Wants to Be Sovereign

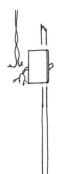

We know that we have some control over what happens. For example, if you want to turn on the lights, you turn on the light switch. Did you make the lights turn on by turning on the light switch? Yes. But what if the light switch broke just before you turned on the light? What if the electricity was cut off to the house just as you turned on the light switch? You see, you cannot be absolutely sure that the lights will turn on when you turn on the light switch. Only God can plan something and cause it to happen with absolute certainty.

We have learned that God is sovereign. But man wants to be sovereign. He wants to be in total control of everything that happens to him. This is called "**humanism**." Sometimes men will make their governments very powerful so that their governments can control what happens in the future. They think that governments can save them from starvation, cure all diseases someday, and take care of all of their problems. But no matter how much power they give to governments, they still cannot solve all of their problems. They cannot foresee all of the things that can go wrong to save themselves from all these problems. In fact, when you give a government lots of power, it makes even more mistakes. It will only make problems worse for the people. We are responsible to obey God. But we must also trust in God to take care of us even as he takes care of the little birds and the lilies of the field (Matthew 6:28-32). God is in control of the future.

Humanism is the idea that man should be sovereign and in control of everything.

KING NEBUCHADNEZZAR

Not only is God in control of dice and birds, but He is also in control of the most powerful men on earth. About 450 years before Christ, the most powerful man on earth was King Nebuchadnezzar in Babylon. Most powerful men are very proud, and this king was one of the most proud kings ever. So to humble this proud king, God made him look and act like a beast. He put him out to pasture to eat grass like the animals.

In Daniel 4, we read of King Nebuchadnezzar's pride:

DANIEL 4:30

The king spoke, saying, "Is not this great Babylon, that I have built for a royal dwelling by my mighty power and for the honor of my majesty?"

But God humbled him:

DANIEL 4:31-32

While the word was still in the king's mouth, a voice fell from heaven: "King Nebuchadnezzar, to you it is spoken: the kingdom has departed from you! And they shall drive you from men, and your dwelling shall be with the beasts of the field. They shall make you eat grass like oxen; and seven times shall pass over you, until you know that the Most High rules in the kingdom of men, and gives it to whomever He chooses."

So you see that old King Nebuchadnezzar learned a lesson. God always rules over the kingdoms of men, and He gives over the power of the kingdom to the people he chooses. Today, the people who vote think that they rule. They think that they are in control over who gets elected, because they get to vote on election day.

But God is in control over everything, including the media and the thoughts that come into every person's mind. If a man named George Bush gets elected, that's because God wanted him elected. If a man named Barack Obama gets elected, that's because God wanted him elected. So you see, God controls the little birds and the powerful presidents. God controls everything.

Chapter 2 Review

Proverbs 16:33

The lot is cast into the lap, but its every decision is from the LORD.

Psalm 146

Praise the LORD!
Praise the LORD, O my soul! While I live I will praise the LORD; I will sing praises to my God while I have my being. Do not put your trust in princes, nor in a son of man, in whom there is no help. His spirit departs, he returns to his earth; in that very day his plans perish. Happy is he who has the God of Jacob for his help, whose hope is in the LORD his God, Who made heaven and earth, the sea, and all that is in them; Who keeps truth forever, Who executes justice for the oppressed,

[continued]

Who gives food to the hungry. The LORD gives freedom to the prisoners. The LORD opens the eyes of the blind; the LORD raises those who are bowed down; the LORD loves the righteous. The LORD watches over the strangers; He relieves the fatherless and widow; but the way of the wicked He turns upside down. The LORD shall reign forever—Your God, O Zion, to all generations. Praise the LORD!

1. Where do cars and houses come from?

_____

2. Who made the materials used to make cars and houses?

_____

3. What would happen if you lit a firecracker in a bowl of sand?

_____

4. When did God create the very first plants and animals? (Hint: See Genesis 1.)

_____

_____

5. When did God create the first man? (Hint: See Genesis 1.)

_____

_____

6. Do volcanoes erupt by chance or by God's direction?

_____

7. What big volcano created some very deep canyons in 1980?

_____

8. What major event formed the continents and the ocean floors?

_____

9. What did God intend to do by bringing the worldwide flood (according to Genesis 7:4)?

_____

_____

_____

10. Give some examples of things that are real but cannot be seen.

_____

_____

11. What is God (according to John 4:24)?

_____

_____

12. How do we know that God is real?

_____

_____

13. What else is real (according to the Bible)?

_____

_____

14. What do we mean when we say that God is sovereign?

_____

_____

15. When you throw dice in a game, does God know what you will roll even before you roll them? How does He know what you will roll?

_____

_____

16. What happened to old King Nebuchadnezzar when he became too proud?

_____

_____

17. What is humanism?

_____

_____

_____

18. Why do men make their civil governments so big and powerful?

_____

_____

_____

Vocabulary

Match the word with the correct definition on the right-hand side of the page.

Universities

Evolved

Accident

Creation

Providence

Preserving

Governing

Philosopher

Revelation

Reality

Sovereign

Vote

Election

Certainty

The making known of a secret or the unknown

Develop gradually, especially from a simple to a more complex form

Maintain (something) in its original or existing state

Possessing supreme or ultimate power

The world or the state of things as they actually exist

The action or process of bringing something into existence

An incident that happens by chance (nothing causes it)

The work of God caring for his creation

Ruling

The quality of being reliably true

A person engaged or learned in philosophy, esp. as an academic discipline

Choosing somebody to rule over you

Schools offering advanced teaching (after you graduate from high school)

The process of electing people to rule over you

Crossword Puzzle

Across

2. The study of moral principles, right and wrong

3. A value or principle that is always true or right

5. God created the heavens and the_____.

9. The Study of Truth

10. Something that no one meant to happen

11. God made him on the 6th day.

12. The part of us that is sensitive to right and wrong

14. To firmly decide

Down

1. The Study of Reality

4. God making everything of nothing

6. Killing a child in its mother's womb

7. Not fake or imaginary

8. God gave ten of these

13. Dried up or withered

Note: Use vocabulary from Chapters 1, 2, and 3 for this excercise.

Chapter 3

Ethics: What's the Big Idea Here?

" **Matthew 22:37-38**

Jesus said to him, 'You shall love the LORD your God with all your heart, with all your soul, and with all your mind.' This is the first and great commandment.

What's the Big Idea Here?

In the first chapter, we described worldviews as glasses through which you see everything around you. Here is another way to understand this idea of worldviews. Most children ask a lot of questions. They ask questions because they are curious about the world around them. Perhaps you too have asked your parents a few questions. There are very many questions to ask. Here are some examples:

What is the capital of Turkey?
How do you make glass?
Why do dogs bark?
What's for dinner tonight?
Does God exist?

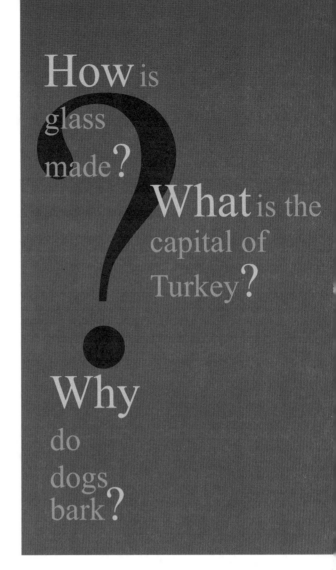

From this list of questions, you may notice that not all questions are really important. Some questions are really big and important questions, and some are really small and unimportant questions. The question "What's for dinner tonight?" is less important than the question "Does God exist?" Of course you would like to know what's for dinner tonight because the answer to that question will affect you and your tummy tonight! But most people in the world don't really care what you will have for dinner tonight. However, the question "Does God exist?" affects everything in your life and

The question "Does God exist?" affects everything in your life and everything in everybody else's life. That's why it is such a big question.

everything in everybody else's life. That's why it is such a big question. Your world-view is a collection of all the answers to the big questions. There are three big questions, or three categories of questions, that people ask. They are:

What is true? What is the basis for truth?

How do we know something is true?

What is real? Is God real? Am I real? Is this world real?

Where did this world come from?

Is there right and wrong? What is right and wrong?

These questions address the areas of epistemology (the study of truth), metaphysics (the study of reality), and ethics (the study of right and wrong). Up to this point in our study course, we have looked at the first two areas, epistemology and metaphysics. This chapter will consider the third: ethics.

Epistemology, metaphysics, and ethics are pretty big words. Do you think you can remember what they mean?

Right and Wrong, Good and Evil

When it comes to this subject of ethics, there are two different things you need to understand:

Right and Wrong

First, there is right and wrong. This has to do with your actions. There are some actions that are right actions and there are some that are wrong actions. Can you name some right actions and some wrong actions? We all agree that robbing a bank is a wrong thing to do. And we also agree that helping a poor orphan by adopting him into your family might be a right thing to do.

Good and Evil

Secondly, there is good and evil. Sometimes this is the consequence of your actions. If you hit your brother in anger (which would be a wrong thing to do), you give him a bloody nose, which is evil. If you give your brother a gift (which might be a right thing to do), he is blessed, and that is good. But good and evil also have to do with how things are going with us. Sickness and death are evil things, for example. Have you ever been sick? Do you enjoy being sick? What if somebody was to come to you and say, "You did the wrong thing by catching the measles. You are an evil person!" In this case, catching the disease is not a sin or a wrong thing to do. But the disease itself is an evil thing.

What Is Right and Wrong?

Almost everybody believes that there are certain things that are the right things to do, and there are certain things that are the wrong things to do. Nowadays there are people that will try to tell you that there is no absolute right and wrong. But if somebody steals something from them, they get very upset. They stomp around and tell everybody that this stealing business is all wrong. If somebody tells them that the ice on a lake is thick enough to keep them from falling through, they become very upset with the liar when they fall through thin ice in the middle of the lake.

This is because every human being has a sense for right and wrong. The Bible calls this a "conscience." Your conscience makes you feel bad when you have done something wrong. If you disobey your mom, your conscience will bother you, and you will feel guilty until you ask for forgiveness. Many people's consciences are seared. Over the years they have learned how to ignore the cries of their conscience within them so they don't feel very bad when they sin. These people are hardened in their sin.

> ## Genesis 3:6
>
> So when the woman saw that the tree was good for food, that is was pleasant to the eyes, and a tree desirable to make one wise, she took of its fruit and ate. She also gave to her husband with her, and he ate.

We also learn from the Bible that we have another problem. At the beginning, man fell into sin. Man was good when God created him. He always did the right thing. But then Adam (the first man) did the wrong thing. He disobeyed God when He told him not to eat of a certain tree. Do you remember this from the first chapter? This created a big problem. This problem made people believe that doing the wrong thing was the right thing to do! The mind and conscience of men were damaged by that first sin. So the conscience doesn't work as well as it used to before Adam fell into sin.

There Is Such a Thing as Right and Wrong

There are some people who tell us that there is no such thing as right and wrong. This is another example of how people's minds have been corrupted by the fall of Adam. If there were no right and wrong, then we could not condemn very evil people like Adolf Hitler or Nero. These evil leaders killed many people without cause. But why are they evil? What makes something right and something else wrong? Why is it wrong to murder somebody else? Why would it be wrong to rob a bank? Is there a way to find out what is right and what is wrong? How do we answer these important questions?

> If there were no right and wrong, then we could not condemn very evil people like Adolf Hitler or Nero. These evil leaders killed many people without cause.

Almost everybody will agree that there is good and there is evil. But many people cannot agree on what is right and what is wrong. They change their opinions very often on what is good and what is evil.

For example, many Germans thought that Adolf Hitler was a wonderful leader in 1940. Today most, if not all, of the German people believe he was an evil man. Human beings cannot agree on who the evil people are and who the good people are. This is because their minds became messed up when Adam fell into sin.

How Can We Tell What Is Good and What Is Evil?

You must see the importance of this question. If you don't know what is good and evil, or right and wrong, then you might do the wrong things and live your life as a very evil person. If the police and judges are mixed up on this, they might punish the good people who do right things and reward the evil people who do evil things. Let us try to answer this question. How do we tell what is good and what is evil? There are several possible answers.

1 One way to try to answer that question is to use our consciences (that part of our minds that makes us feel bad when we do something wrong). The conscience can be helpful. But it is not very reliable because of man's sinful condition. Our minds play tricks on us. So this method doesn't work.

2 Suppose we were to ask one hundred people whether it is right to rob banks. What if 51 of them said "Sure!" Would that make it right to rob banks? As we pointed out earlier, people's opinions change all of the time. Also, their opinions are usually formed by a few powerful people who own the television news stations and control the schools. If these powerful people who tell millions of people what to believe are evil people, then the people may come to believe wrong things. Sadly, we see this happening very often in our nation today. So you can see that this is not a good way to decide if something is right or wrong.

3 Here's another idea. Maybe we should tell everybody to do the things that will make themselves happy. The trouble with this is that some people are happy when they hurt others. If we only do those things that make ourselves happy, then we do not care about the happiness of others. We would become big selfish pigs. Another problem is that we don't know what would make us happy. So this is not helpful either.

4 Or maybe we should tell everybody to do the things that would make other people happy, and that would bless them. This idea is a little better than the last one. But we still have the same problem: nobody knows what sorts of things will make some people happy without making other people unhappy! We may do things in the hope that others will be happy and blessed. However, making people happy may not be good for them. If you gave a little four-year-old one hundred pounds of candy, it might make him happy. But it might also make him very sick. So this is also a bad way to think about right and wrong.

The problem with all four of these answers is that men rely on themselves to determine what is right and what is wrong. This is called "humanism." When men want to decide what is right and wrong, they have turned themselves into gods. They try to replace God with themselves. The problem with humanism is that God is the only one who has the power to decide what is right and what is wrong. It is not for us to determine this. Those people that want to make their own list of commandments are trying to become "god." Humanism turns man into his own god.

Only God knows for sure what is right and wrong since He determines right and wrong.

The best way to find out what is right and what is wrong is to go to God's revelation in the Bible. Only God knows for sure what is right and wrong since He determines right and wrong. So we should ask Him what is right and wrong! If you look into the Bible, you will discover right away that God has much to say about what is right and what is wrong. In fact, God gave Moses the Ten Commandments when he was up on Mount Sinai. They were not just ten suggestions. They were ten commandments.

Jesus said to him, "'You shall love the LORD your God with all your heart, with all your soul, and with all your mind.' This is the first and great commandment. And the second is like it: 'You shall love your neighbor as yourself.' On these two commandments hang all the Law and the Prophets."

Matthew 22:37-40

Love Is Always the Right Thing to Do.

Love is always the right thing to do. Again, almost everyone agrees with this. But love means different things to different people. So we must answer two important questions. Who are we supposed to love? And what is love? The Bible gives us some direction on this. First, we're supposed to love God, and we are supposed to love our neighbor as ourselves. Secondly, we love God and love our neighbor by keeping God's commandments.

In the 1960s, a popular rock and roll band called "The Beatles" sang a song called "All You Need Is Love." Almost everybody agrees with this. Even Jesus said the whole law is summarized in one command: love God.

When the Beatles rock band said, "All you need is love," they did not mean what Jesus meant by love. Everyone agrees that love is a good thing. But they do not define love the way that God defines it. We love God *by* keeping His commandments. We love our neighbor *by* keeping God's commandments. If men's hearts were right, they could obey the commandment to love, and they would always be doing the right thing. But their

> We love God *by* keeping His commandments. We love our neighbor *by* keeping God's commandments.

hearts are corrupted, and so the laws of God help them to define love. These laws show them all of the ways in which they do not love God and their neighbor.

The Whole Bible Teaches About Right and Wrong

The Bible gives many instructions to help us understand if something is right or wrong. For example, some people think that it is wrong to purposefully kill a baby in a crib, but it is okay to kill the baby when it is in its mommy's womb. Well, does God consider that child to be a real person in the womb?

As you know, the sixth commandment tells us not to murder people. But what about the baby in his mommy's womb? You will find that Psalm 139:13-16 and Psalm 22:10 refer to the child as a special little person in relationship to God. That means the child in its mommy's womb is a person, so it would be just as bad to purposefully kill him when he is in the womb as it would be to kill him in the crib.

The Bible has many important laws to help us tell the difference between the right things to do and the wrong things to do. Here are some examples:

Should you pay your pastors if your pastors work hard at bringing messages to you?

Paul has something to say about this in **1 Timothy 5:17-18.** Look up these verses to discover what God says is the right thing to do.

If your house had a really high porch where people enjoyed barbeques (twenty feet off of the ground), what do you think God would want you to do to protect people from falling off the porch? Actually, God's law has something to say about this in **Deuteronomy 22:8.** Look up this Bible verse to find out what God says is the right thing to do.

Occasionally, there are boys who want to wear girls' clothes. Does God's law have anything to say about this in **Deuteronomy 22:5**?

As you can see, the Bible addresses every aspect of life. Sometimes, we have to think about it for a while in order to understand what God wants us to do with our high porches and boys who wear girls' clothes. But God has something to say about everything, and we need to learn the whole Bible so we can learn how to love God by keeping His commandments.

Chapter 3 Review

Scripture Reading

**Exodus 20:1-17
(The Ten Commandments)**

And God spoke all these words, saying. . .

You shall have no other gods before Me.

You shall not make for yourself a carved image—any likeness of anything that is in heaven above, or that is in the earth beneath, or that is in the water under the earth; you shall not bow down to them nor serve them. For I, the LORD your God, am a jealous God, visiting the iniquity of the fathers upon the children to the third and fourth generations of those who hate Me, but showing mercy to thousands, to those who love Me and keep My commandments.

You shall not take the name of the LORD your God in vain, for the LORD will not hold him guiltless who takes His name in vain.

Remember the Sabbath day, to keep it holy. Six days you shall labor and do all your work, but the seventh day is the Sabbath of the LORD your God. In it you shall do no work: you, nor your son, nor your daughter, nor your male servant, nor your female servant, nor your cattle, nor your stranger who is within your gates. For in six days the LORD made the heavens and the earth, the sea, and all that is in them, and rested the seventh day. Therefore the LORD blessed the Sabbath day and hallowed it.

Honor your father and your mother, that your days may be long upon the land which the LORD your God is giving you.

You shall not murder.

You shall not commit adultery.

You shall not steal.

You shall not bear false witness against your neighbor.

You shall not covet your neighbor's house; you shall not covet your neighbor's wife, nor his male servant, nor his female servant, nor his ox, nor his donkey, nor anything that is your neighbor's.

1. Which question is a bigger question: "What's for dinner tonight?" or "Does God exist?"

_____

2. How is "worldview" defined in this chapter?

_____

_____

3. What are the three big questions?

_____

_____

_____

4. Which of the following are wrong things, and which are simply evil things that happen to you? (Put "W" next to the wrong things, and "E" next to the evil or bad things that happen to you.)

__ Catching a cold
__ Stealing a candy bar
__ Lying to your parents
__ Tripping on a big rock and skinning your knee
__ Falling in a river and drowning
__ Throwing a rock in anger at your brother
__ Accidentally riding your bike into your friend
__ Carelessly hitting a ball into your neighbor's glass door

5. How does your conscience make you feel when you do something bad?

_____

6. What happens to men who have hard hearts and seared consciences?

_____

_____

7. What was Adam like when he was first created (in the moral sense)? Was he good or evil?

_____

8. How did Adam commit the first sin against God?

_____

_____

9. If people cannot agree on what is good and evil, or who is right and who is wrong, then how can we figure out these things? How can we ever know for sure what is a good thing to do, and what is a bad thing to do?

_____

_____

10. What if you decided that you would do whatever makes you happy? What would be the problem with this?

_____

_____

11. How many commandments did God give to Moses on the mountain?

_____

12. Which of the ten commandments mentions family members?

_____

13. Who are we supposed to love, according to Jesus?

_____

14. How do we love God and love our neighbors according to the
Bible?_____

_____

15. What verse in the Bible talks about paying pastors who work very hard
in the church? _____

16. What should you do if you have a really high porch (20 feet off of
the ground) according to Deuteronomy 22:8?

_____

_____

17. What does the Bible say about boys who want to wear girls'
clothes (Deuteronomy 22:5)?

_____

_____

18. Which two of the ten commandments have to do with your
speech? What do these commandments forbid?

_____

_____

19. What does the Bible say about little babies in their mothers'
wombs (Psalm 139:13-16, Psalm 22:10)?

_____

When God gave these commandments to the nation of Israel, He intended them to be used by everyone, everywhere, and for all time. They are absolute laws that would be wrong to disobey. These ten laws are the foundation for all of the other laws that God gave Israel. In the same way, they are the foundation of all the laws that we should use to govern our societies and ourselves.

Some of the Ten Commandments tell us about how we love God by relating to Him, and some tell us how we love God by relating to our neighbors. **Write the ones relating to God on the left tablet and the ones relating to our neighbors on the right tablet.**

Vocabulary

Match the word with the correct definition on the right-hand side of the page.

Ethics	The part of us that is sensitive to right and wrong
Absolute	A value or principle that is always true or right
Conscience	Killing a child in its mother's womb
Seared	The study of truth. What is true?
Metaphysics	Burnt or dried up
Epistemology	To firmly decide
Determine	The study of reality. What is real?
Abortion	The study of moral principles (right and wrong)

Chapter 4

The Study of You

"

Ephesians 2:5-6

But God, who is rich in mercy, because of His great love with which He loved us, even when we were dead in trespasses, made us alive together with Christ (by grace you have been saved), and raised us up together, and made us sit together in the heavenly places in Christ Jesus.

The Study of You

In this chapter, we want to talk about you. I'm sure that you know that you are not alone on this globe. You were not created to be alone. In fact, when man was first created, God said, "It is not good for man to be alone." So He created a woman for the man. In this world, there is you, and then there are other people.

This chapter will deal with the study of you. This is called **"anthropology."**

You

Look at yourself for a moment. What are you? You are not a plant. You cannot swim under the water like a fish. You cannot fly through the air like a bird. What are you? Are you some kind of an advanced species of ape that has learned to walk on your two back legs? The Bible is clear on this issue. You are a human being, created in the image of God.

> In this world, there is you, and then there are other people.

So God created man in His own image; in the image of God He created him; male and female He created them.

Genesis 1:27

From this passage, we discover that there are two kinds of people in the world: boys and girls (or men and women). Both of them are created in God's image. Later, we will learn that God made men and women so that together they can build families.

The Differences Between God and You

There are some differences between God and you. The most obvious difference is that God creates things out of nothing. God made you, and you cannot create things like God can. God is also sovereign, which means that He controls everything that happens in this world. This includes every sparrow that falls from the sky and every president who is elected. Of course, you are not in control of these things. Are you in control of every sparrow that falls to the ground?

> Can you make a sparrow fall to the ground? Of course you cannot. God is all-powerful, and He is in control of everything that happens.

Could you make sure that an earthquake misses one city and disrupts another city? Of course you can't. God is all-powerful, and He is in control of everything that happens. God knows everything, and He is present everywhere.

There is a second very obvious difference between God and you. God is invisible. You cannot see God because He is Spirit. Have you ever tried to make yourself invisible? Of course, that is impossible because you are made up of both body and spirit. Every person is made of these two things. Your body is a physical form that you can feel and see. Your spirit is the invisible part of you.

Westminster Shorter Catechism

Question 4: What is God?

God is a Spirit, infinite, eternal, unchangeable, in His being, wisdom, power, holiness, justice, goodness, and truth.

When you die, your physical body remains, but there is no longer a living spirit within you. A living person cannot possibly separate his body and spirit. You cannot sit on a chair and send your spirit over to the other side of the room.

The Similarities Between God and You

But there are also similarities between God and you. For example, you can think. You can love other people like your brothers and sisters or daddy and mommy. You can communicate ideas by speaking with words and sentences. That is something that animals cannot do. You are also a moral creature. If you were to get angry and kill somebody, you would feel very bad about it. You would feel guilt. This is a characteristic that apes and monkeys do not share with you. Baboons and langurs are known to kill within their "troops," and certainly they do not feel any pang of guilt for doing this. But, you feel guilty when you do wrong because you are morally accountable to your Creator. This cannot be said for animals because they are "amoral."

Your conscience is what makes you feel guilty when you sin.

This is why people who do not believe in God also believe that we are like the animals. They would say that guilt is only something that you learn from your parents or from your society. "Your parents make you feel bad when you disappoint them," they say. "There is really nothing wrong with killing somebody. You may disappoint others around you who do not like killing." If there is no God, then there is nothing wrong with killing people. As you can see, this is a very dangerous way of looking at the world. People who do not believe in God are dangerous people.

But the Bible tells us why we feel bad when we do wrong things. We feel guilt because we have broken God's law. If we had only broken a law of some human being, we would not feel that bad about it. But because we break the law of the great

Creator of the Universe, of course we will feel very bad about it. As soon as Adam broke God's rule in the Garden of Eden, he felt very bad about it and tried to hide from God.

What's the Big Problem?

Some people called "Marxists" believe that the Big Problem with human beings is that some people are richer than others. They tell us that we can solve the problem if a powerful government will take money away from the rich people and give it to the poor people so that everybody has the same amount of money.

Many people believe that the Big Problem with human beings is that they are ignorant. They believe that if we can get everybody educated well in schools and colleges, then we can fix that problem. That is why they are always trying to get more government money to pay for big, expensive schools.

Almost everybody in the world knows that there is something wrong with us. We have big problems. But we disagree on the nature of the problem. Everyone has a theory about the Big Problem that we all have to deal with, and what it will take to solve that problem. But man's problem is more than lack of money and ignorance. If you look around, you will find people who hate each other and say nasty things to each other. Some people will even get so angry they will kill another person, like Cain did to Abel. Perhaps you have heard of men who steal money from banks. These people who do these bad things may be very smart, and they may have a lot of money. So you can see how the problems we face in our world are not ignorance or poverty. What is our problem here? The answer to this question is easy if you read the Bible. But many smart people who teach in colleges do not like to read the Bible.

They don't get their answers from the Bible. They say that the problem is "society." "It is the parents' fault that the children do bad things," they say. Or they blame it on television programs, or the schools, or past generations (grandparents and great- grandparents).

There are many other theories on our Big Problem, but we must go to God's Word to figure this one out. As we have said before, God is the only one who can answer the big questions. And our Big Question now is this: "WHAT IS YOUR BIG PROBLEM?"

For all have sinned and come short of the glory of God.

Romans 3:23

The wages of sin is death.

Romans 6:23

Your big problem is sin.

Death is a problem. Disease is a problem. Ignorance is a problem. Often, poverty and starvation are serious problems. But the Big Problem is none of these things. Your Big Problem, as well as everyone else's Big Problem, is sin! According to John, sin is the breaking of the law of God (1 John 3:4). Every other problem in the world comes from this Big Problem. We are all sinners who break God's laws.

Whoever commits sin also commits lawlessness, and sin is lawlessness.

1 John 3:4

But why do we do the bad things that we do? Why do we break God's laws? Is it because we learned how to be bad from our parents or from our friends? Or was there another problem working in us? Jesus explains where all these sins come from in Mark 7:

And He said, "What comes out of a man, that defiles a man. For from within, out of the heart of men, proceed evil thoughts, adulteries, fornications, murders, thefts, covetousness, wickedness, deceit, lewdness, an evil eye, blasphemy, pride, foolishness. All these evil things come from within and defile a man."

Mark 7:20-23

Sometimes a book, a television program, or a friend might influence you to do something bad. But the problem is that your heart wanted to do something bad anyway. It was just that the television program pointed to some specific bad thing you could do. The main reason why you do bad things is that your heart is bad.

Matthew 1:21

And she will bring forth a Son, and you shall call His name Jesus, for He will save His people from their sins.

So how do you fix this problem? Well, first of all, the solution to this problem is not found in government. It is not found in big, expensive schools. The real solution to this problem is found in a Savior, who is the Lord Jesus Christ. When the angel announced Jesus' birth, he told Joseph, "You shall call his name Jesus, for He shall save His people from their sins." (Matthew 1:21).

71

Jesus Christ is the Son of God who became a human being (like you and me). He suffered and died on the cross for our sins. Then He rose again on the third day in victory over death. Through Him, we believe that we will also conquer sin and death!

Jesus Christ came to save us from our sins and the consequences of our sin. He came to save our souls and our bodies from spiritual and physical death. He came to save us from our guilty feelings about the bad things we do. He paid for our sins so that we will not have to pay for them. He also came to save us from doing those bad things.

As you trust in Him as your Savior, you will find that He will change your life. When He changes your life, He will change everything about you. He improves your relationships with your parents. He takes away the sin that messes up our marriages, our businesses, and our governments. This is called sanctification.

The Four Stations in the Journey of Man

Think of the whole history of man as a journey on a train with four stops or four stations: Eden, Fallen City, Gospel Town, and Gloryville. Where are you in this journey?

Station 1: Eden

It all began with Adam back in the Garden of Eden. This was the first station. It was a beautiful garden, and Adam and Eve did not suffer from disease and death. They were without sin. But they were given a choice to obey God or to disobey Him. When they ate the forbidden fruit, they fell into sin. Then God removed them from the garden.

Station 2: Fallen City

This is the second stop for the train ride through history. When man fell into sin, he was very miserable. He suffered from guilt and shame with all of the consequences of sin. The Bible calls him "dead" in his sins (Ephesians 2:1). His mind was damaged badly by the fall. Without God's saving help, he wandered in darkness. He worshiped idols and came up with foolish, hair-brained explanations for the world. As people wandered further away from God and His Word, they turned to many lies. Some of them believed in the lie of evolution. Some believed in the lies of witchcraft. This is the condition in which all of us were born, including you. Some people will never make it out of this station into Gospel Town and Gloryville. Sadly, they will die in their sins and suffer eternal death in hell. But thanks be to God, there is a way out of this dark city as the train of mankind travels into Gospel Town.

Station 3: Gospel Town

When we believe in Jesus who came to save us from our sins, we arrive at the Gospel Station. This is where Jesus Christ the Son of God died on the cross and rose again on the third day. We still have problems with sin, diseases, and even death. But God gives the power to overcome these things piece by piece. By God's grace, we are able to repent of our sins and receive God's forgiveness. We become part of God's family and learn to love our brothers and sisters.

Station 4: Gloryville

Our final destination is Gloryville. After we die, and God raises us from the dead, we will be made perfect. This means that we will never again fall into sin or suffer any consequences of sin like disease or death. This is a better place to be than Eden because we will never have to worry about the possibility of sin or death.

1. Where in the Bible does it say that man was not created to be alone?

_____

2. What are the two parts of you that make you a human being?

_____

3. What are some differences between God and you?

_____

_____

4. What are some similarities between God and you?

_____

_____

5. Do animals feel guilt? Why do you feel guilt?

_____

_____

6. What is the Big Problem with all the people in the world according to the Bible?

_____

7. What are the big problems with the world according to humanists who do not believe the Bible?

_____

_____

8. Read Romans 6:23. What are the wages (payments) required by sin?

_____

_____

9. Describe what a person is like in each of the four stations in "the journey of man."

Station #1 - Eden _____

_____

Station #2 - Fallen City _____

_____

Station #3 - Gospel Town _____

_____

Station #4 - Gloryville _____

_____

10. Of the four stations in the journey of man, where are you in this journey?

_____

_____

11. What is sin (according to 1 John 3:4)?

_____

12. Where does sin come from (according to Jesus in Mark 7:20-23)?

_____

13. Who is Jesus Christ?

_____

14. Why did Jesus come to earth, according to Matthew 1:21?

_____

15. List some things in our lives that change when we trust in Jesus Christ as Savior.

_____

_____

Vocabulary

Match the word with the correct definition on the right-hand side of the page.

Anthropology

Sociology

Disappoint

Guilt

Characteristic

Accountable

Poverty

Influence

Advanced

The feeling you get when you've done something bad

The state of being poor

Tempting or encouraging a person to do something (good or bad)

A feature of quality describing somebody or something

The study of you (man)

Higher levels of complexity

To fail to fulfill the hopes or expectations of (someone)

The study of your relationship with other people in the world

Being responsible to obey somebody

Vocabulary

Match the word with the correct definition on the right-hand side of the page.

Species

Image

Disrupt

Obvious

Invisible

Similar

Consequences

Sanctification

Easily perceived or understood

The results of an action, sometimes a punishment for an action

A representation of something or somebody else

A type of animal or mammal

Moral improvement, becoming holy

To interrupt by causing a disturbance or a problem

The state of having similarities or sharing the same characteristics

Without physical form and impossible to see with the eyes

The Train Game

Ride the train of the journey of man. Look up these scripture passages and write the reference in the station that it applies to.

Genesis 2:17
Ephesians 4:13
Romans 3:23
Genesis 3:6
1 Corinthians 15:42-44
Acts 17:32
Ephesians 2:2-3
Genesis 1:26-27
John 3:16-17
Genesis 3:17
Romans 6:23
Genesis 1:31
Revelation 21:1-5
Ephesians 2:6
Colossians 3:9-10
Ecclesiastes 7:29
Ephesians 2:2-3
1 Corinthians 15:1-4
Isaiah 53:6

Station 1: Eden

Station 2: Fallen City

Station 3: Gospeltown

Station 4: Gloryville

5 Your Community

Proverbs 29:2

When the righteous are in authority, the people rejoice; but when a wicked man rules, the people groan.

Your Community

Now, let us look at your relationship with other people. As you look around, you will probably notice that there are other people in this world, and you must relate to these people! But how do you relate to them?

God the Creator invented three kinds of human organizations. We invent organizations all of the time. For example, we might organize a neighborhood baseball team. Some people start businesses. But God has come up with three special kinds of **organizations** that are very essential for human life.

> As you look around, you will notice that there are other people in this world, and you must relate to these people!

But from the beginning of the creation God made them male and female. For this cause shall a man leave his father and mother, and cleave to his wife; and the two shall be one flesh: so then they are no more two, but one flesh. What therefore God hath joined together, let not man put asunder.

Mark 10:6-9

And I also say to you that you are Peter, and on this rock I will build My church, and the gates of Hades shall not prevail against it.

Matthew 16:18

Let every soul be subject to the governing authorities. For there is no authority except from God, and the authorities that exist are appointed by God. . .For rulers are not a terror to good works, but to evil. . . For he is God's minister to you for good. But if you do evil, be afraid; for he does not bear the sword in vain; for he is God's minister, an avenger to execute wrath on him who practices evil.

Romans 13:1-4

What the Guys in Charge Are Called

The three organizations that God came up with are **family**, **church**, and **state** (or government). Each of these is a kind of government. There are people who are in charge of these organizations. The table below matches the organization with the titles of those who are in charge of those organizations.

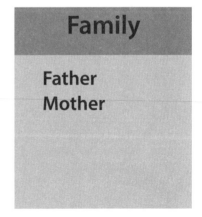

State	Church	Family
President	Pastor	Father
Governor	Elder	Mother
Senator	Deacon	
Judge		

There are several ways to look at these organizations and how they relate to each other. Take a look at the two drawings below:

The Humanist Worldview vs. the Christian Worldview

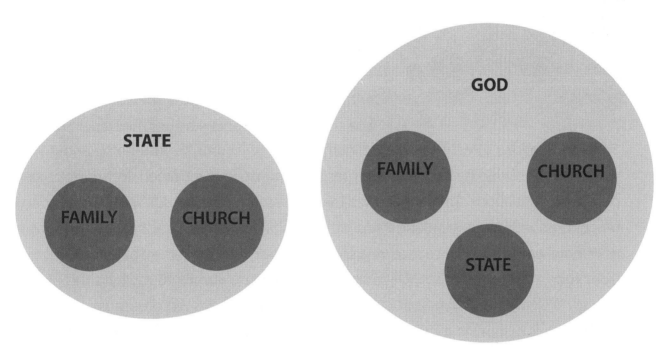

With the humanist worldview, you can see that the state (or civil government) is everything. From this perspective, the state (or the civil government) allows the family and the church to operate within its realm. The state has all the power. But with the Christian worldview, you can see that God has all power. God is in total control. He created the family, the church, and the state, and He allows them to operate within His rule.

You can see that there is a big battle between these two ideas. The one side thinks that the state is all powerful. The other side believes that God is all powerful. We insist that God gives everybody their authority to operate. A father and mother cannot do whatever they want to do, and presidents cannot do whatever they want to do. God tells them how much power they get. Otherwise they will step on the rights and the authority of others.

Here is an example that will help you to understand this concept. As you know, there are problems in our society with undisciplined children. Perhaps you have seen them at the supermarket. They yell, scream, and throw groceries around the store. Now, if these children get to be adults, you know they will still be undisciplined. They will not honor authority. They will be lazy and destructive. So what do we do about this problem of "bratty" children? A government official might come up with a solution to this problem. He suggests that the state governments start up the Department of Spanking Children. Every day, the spanking police will come to your home and give you a well-deserved paddling. These spanking police will be trained according to department regulations. They are trained in the Spanking Manual. Each spanking police officer is issued a nice Spanking Paddle that is built to certain specifications. Alright now, how would you like to receive a spanking every day from the Spanking Police from your state government? Of course, this is all just plain silly. But why is this all wrong? Well, we need to go back to God's instructions in His Word because they will tell us who is responsible for disciplining children. Read the following verse carefully.

He who spares his rod hates his son, but he who loves him disciplines him promptly.

Proverbs 13:24

Now as you read this text, who do you think is responsible for disciplining a son? Is it the responsibility of the Spanking Police from the state government? Of course not. It is a father's responsibility because God gave that responsibility to the family.

God assigns certain responsibilities to families. He assigns certain responsibilities to the church and others to the state.

The trouble comes when one of these spheres tries to take over everything. Suppose your father decided that he would personally punish all of the thieves and murderers in your state, so he strapped a .45 caliber handgun to his waist and went around the cities shooting the bad guys. I hope you can see a problem with this! Of course, your father is head of his family. He is responsible to take care of his family, but it is not his responsibility to shoot all of the bad guys in town. That responsibility lies with the civil government.

Sometimes the church tries to control the state. This happened during the 1300s and 1400s in Europe. But most of the time the state tries to control the church and the family. This is what has happened since the 1600s in Europe and America.

If you live in America, you may remember the reason why the Pilgrims came here in the 1620s. One of the main reasons was freedom to choose their own pastors. There was a very good Christian pastor named John Bunyan. This man wrote some great books like *Pilgrim's Progress* and *The Holy War*. He wrote most of his books while he was sitting in jail. He would preach the Word of God without a license from the state, so eventually the king's men threw John into prison. For most of the 1600s, the state was trying to control the church. For example, if the king's men did not like a pastor in your church, they would tell you to get rid of him so they could bring in their own man to teach the Bible and serve the Lord's Supper in the way that they saw fit. This is why the Pilgrims came to America. First they had escaped to Holland, and then they came to America for freedom. They wanted the church to operate without the state interfering with their worship.

What happens when the state takes upon itself the authority to control and boss around the church? The Pilgrims and Puritans that came to America were very concerned that if the state controlled the church, then it would end up destroying the church. This is what happened in places like England and Germany over the years.

But now the problem is just as bad (or maybe even worse) in countries all over the world. The civil government is not as interested in controlling the church any more. Since the 1800s and 1900s, the national governments have worked very hard to take control over the family. By the year 1920, they captured control of the education of most of the children in those countries. Then by the 1930s our governments began to pay for the care of the elderly parents and grandparents. Later in the 1960s and 1970s, the big governments started to provide houses and food for poor people. These poor people did not need fathers any more to take care of their families. So the fathers left their homes and never came back. Now about 70% of these poor children are born without fathers. Most of them will never live with their fathers. This is one of the most horrible things that has ever happened in all of history.

The civil government has worked very hard to take control over the family. But what happens to the family when the government takes over the family?

We have learned that when the government pays for things, it gets control over those things. So the government has tried to take over every aspect of family life in many countries. But when the civil government tries to take over family responsibilities, it destroys families. This is exactly what has happened!

Good Communities

Can you see how your relationships with other people are very important? If you have bad family relationships, or if you live in a nation with a bad government, that just makes your life more miserable.

If God has blessed you with a good family, then you should thank Him for that. If God has blessed you with good churches and good governments that keep the nation safe and free, then you should be thankful for that! Some people are blessed with good strong families and nice communities. Sadly, there are some people that are not blessed with these things. So the Big Question now is this: How would you know if you have a good community? What is it that makes a good community, strong families, and good government?

There are some people who think that the world would be better off without families. They work very hard to destroy the family and make the state very powerful. This was the commitment of the man named Karl Marx. Those who follow Marxist ideas are usually called "socialists." But we believe that the best, the most healthy, and the most blessed communities are those that follow the instructions found in God's Word. When families do what families are supposed to do, churches do what churches are supposed to do, and the civil governments do what they are supposed to do, God will bless your society.

What are families, churches, and states supposed to do? Again, we go back to the Bible. Here is where we find out how to distribute power and responsibilities among families, churches, and states. In the following exercises, you will use the Bible to determine which responsibilities belong to the family, the church, and the state.

> When families do what families are supposed to do, churches do what churches are supposed to do, and the civil governments do what they are supposed to do, God will bless your society!

Chapter 5 Review

Scripture Memory

Proverbs 29:2

When the righteous are in authority, the people rejoice; but when a wicked man rules, the people groan.

Scripture Reading

Mark 10:6-9

But from the beginning of the creation, God 'made them male and female.' 'For this reason a man shall leave his father and mother and be joined to his wife, and the two shall become one flesh'; so then they are no longer two, but one flesh. Therefore what God has joined together, let not man separate."

Matthew 16:18

And I also say to you that you are Peter, and on this rock I will build My church, and the gates of Hades shall not prevail against it.

Romans 13:1-4

Let every soul be subject to the governing authorities. For there is no authority except from God, and the authorities that exist are appointed by God . . .For rulers are not a terror to good works, but to evil. . . For he is God's minister to you for good. But if you do evil, be afraid; for he does not bear the sword in vain; for he is God's minister, an avenger to execute wrath on him who practices evil.

1. Who are the people that are in charge of the family?

_____

2. Who are the people that are in charge of the church?

_____

_____

3. Who are the people that are in charge of the state?

_____

_____

4. According to the humanist worldview, who gets all the power?

_____

5. According to a biblical worldview, who has all the power and authority over the family, the church, and the state?

_____

6. Who is responsible for spanking (or disciplining) children, according to the Bible? Provide a Bible reference for this.

_____

_____

7. Why is it wrong for your father to shoot all of the bad guys in town?

_____

_____

_____

8. Why was it wrong for the state to throw John Bunyan in prison for preaching without a license?

_____

_____

_____

9. What is the big powerful state government trying to control today?

_____

_____

_____

10. What happens to the church when the state tries to control the church? What happens to the family when the state tries to control the family?

_____

_____

_____

_____

11. What do we call people who follow Karl Marx?

_____

12. What was Karl Marx's commitment? What was he trying to do?

_____

_____

_____

_____

Vocabulary

Match the word with the correct definition on the right-hand side of the page.

Community

Organization

Essential

Undisciplined

Government

Regulations

Interfere

Socialists

Church

Family

People who empower the state to solve all their problems for them

Rules

A group of people living together, in relationship with each other

An authority established by God that governs or rules

Not behaving well, disorderly

A body of people from different families that gather to hear God's Word and worship God together

A father, mother, and children (as God provides)

A group of people organized for a specific reason

Vitally important, very important

Getting in the way; trying to rule over something illegitimately

The Umbrella Game

Which of the following belong to family, church, and state?
Record each task under the appropriate umbrella.

Mowing your lawn

Arresting criminals

Teaching children

Baptizing

Spanking children

Defending country

Taking care of elderly parents

Preaching God's Word

Taking care of widows without family

Feeding children

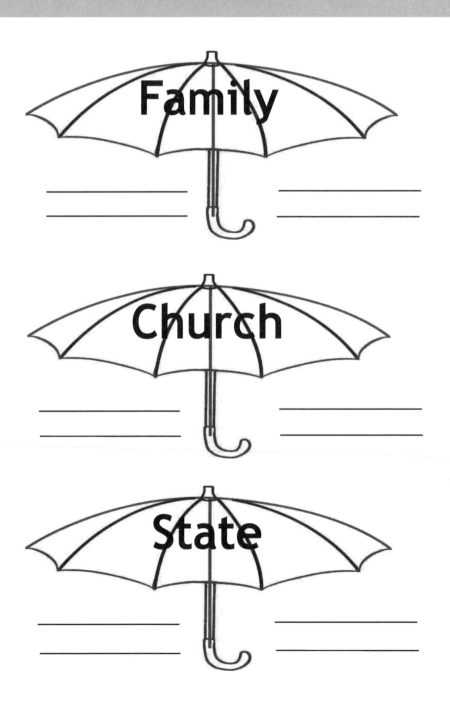

Family

Church

State

Chapter

6 The Family

Mark 10:6-9

But from the beginning of the creation, God 'made them male and female.' 'For this reason a man shall leave his father and mother and be joined to his wife, and the two shall become one flesh'; so then they are no longer two, but one flesh. Therefore what God has joined together, let not man separate.

The Family

Since the 1820s, there have been many changes that have happened in our world. We don't ride around in horse-drawn carriages anymore. We can fly to another continent in just 12 hours or so. We have many wonderful gadgets like refrigerators, cell phones, and computers. Even some of the poorest people have refrigerators in their homes today. This was unheard of one hundred years ago! We have far more wealth and free time to enjoy entertaining shows and amusement parks than those living in the 1820s.

But there are two very important changes that have happened in your world in the last one hundred years that you need to know about:

> **1** **The government has grown very, very powerful.**

> **2** **The family has become very, very weak.**

In the last chapter, we pointed out that the government likes to get more powerful at the expense of the family. But in this chapter we do not want to speak about the government. We want to take a special look at the family.

When we say the family has become very weak, it does not mean that *every* family is weak. Maybe God has blessed your family, and you are doing all right. But if you look at twenty families living in your neighborhood, on average these families are doing far worse than families did one hundred years ago. Most of American families are falling apart.

Dr. James Dobson is a Christian researcher and writer who has studied the American family for the last forty years. Dr. Dobson has written many books on the family.

Recently, he gave his diagnosis on the condition of the family. He said:

> " The greatest tragedy of the 20th century was the breakdown of the family in the West. - *Dr. James Dobson*

Many families are falling apart! Of all those children born in 2009, 41% of the children did not have a father. If you look at a crowd of 100 children at a public school, 41 of them were born without fathers. Back in 1960, only 6% of children were born without fathers. Do you see that this is a very big jump from 6% to 41%?

In the 1800s almost every child would grow up with a daddy and mommy for 18 years. There were only about 4% of marriages that fell apart, because the parents get a divorce. If there were 100 families in your neighborhood, then only four families would be broken. Now almost half of marriages (between 40% and 50%) fall apart.[2]

Today, about 70% of children will not grow up with a daddy and mommy for all 18 years. This is because their daddies and mommies do not get married in the first place, or they get divorced. Nowadays, it is hard to find good, strong families.

[2] Dr. Andrew Cherlin, "Marriage, Divorce, Remarriage" (Harvard Univ. Press, 1981), Sociology professor at Johns Hopkins University

There are homes with people living by themselves. There are homes where a mommy lives with her children. There are homes where a man lives with a man. There are homes where a woman lives with a woman. But it is hard to find normal families where a daddy, a mommy, and children live together (in what is called the "nuclear family"). These homes make up less than one-half of American households.

Now this is horrible news for families and for children as well. But many of our leaders in schools and government don't care about this. They are happy that the family is falling apart. Many of them don't think it is a big deal. The family is not important to them, and the government (or the state) is VERY important to them. But the family is much more important to Christians. We are very sad that the world has destroyed the family.

Why Is the Family Important to Us?

Why is the family important to us? Now that is a good question. If the family is not important to the world around us, why is the family so important to us? Well, we should ask the same question we have asked all along in this course. *What does the Bible say about that?* What does the Bible say about the family?

But from the beginning of the creation God 'made them male and female.' 'For this cause shall a man leave his father and mother, and cleave to his wife; and the two shall be one flesh'; so then they are no more two, but one flesh. What therefore God has joined together, let not man put asunder.

Mark 10:6-9

For the LORD God of Israel says that He hates divorce.

Malachi 2:16

The oneness of the family is very important to God. He does not want anybody breaking the family apart.

> The *oneness* of the family means that it acts as one unit, even though it is made up of more than one person (see Mark 10:8).

Exercise

Take two pieces of cardboard and glue them together with a heavy-duty wood glue. Let the cardboard dry. Now try to rip the two pieces of cardboard apart. Do you see how it is impossible to get a clean separation of the two pieces of cardboard? When you get married, you're not supposed to take the marriage apart. Once you have brought the two together, you cannot take them apart without hurting people in that family. You see, God has designed the family as a unit.

There is one more passage from the Bible that you need to know about. The apostle Paul gives a list of qualifications for men who serve as elders in the church.

A bishop then must be. . . one who rules his own house well, having his children in submission with all reverence, (for if a man does not know how to rule his own house, how will he take care of the church of God?)

1 Timothy 3:4-5

The family and the church should make up about 90-95% of a biblical social system. The family and the church are more important than the state government for Christians who follow the Bible. The family is the basic building block of the church, because the church is made up of different families. Who should be put in charge of leading the church? According to 1 Timothy 3:4-5, the church leaders must be men who have learned how to lead their own families well. But if families are weaker than ever today, how are we going to have strong churches? Do you see how good, strong families are important for strong churches?

Do you see how good, strong families are important for strong churches?

How Did Families Get to Be So Weak?

So how did we get into the mess that we are in? Well, the breakdown of the family came several ways. Let's look at several of the bombs that destroyed the family in our countries.

1   The Government Bomb

Do you remember the last lesson on family, church, and state? Sometimes the government does what the family is supposed to do. This is exactly what has happened. The government raises children in schools. Parents do not feel that they are responsible for their children's training and education, so they hand their kids over to the government in the first grade, or in kindergarten, or even in pre-school. Sometimes the government even feeds the children. This teaches a child that the government is more important than the family. It teaches a child that the government is supposed to raise children. They learn the lesson well. So when children grow up, they don't feel like they need to raise their own children. The government has weakened the family.

2   The Fornication Bomb

The word "fornication" is a big word. It is breaking the 7th commandment. This sin happens when boys and girls have relationships with each other that are not appropriate. It is very common today. Sometimes boys and girls go on dates together, but they have no intention to get married. They want to enjoy the blessings of marriage, but they don't want to get married. This is a big problem, and many babies are born to parents who are not married to each other. This has done a lot to ruin the family.

3   The "It's All About Me" Bomb

We live in a very selfish age today. Young people just want to have fun. They do not want to take on responsibility. From the time they were children, they thought life was just fun and games. When they were growing up, they didn't learn to work hard and serve others in the home. Maybe they were laying around the house, watching television, and eating junk food. Of course, as these young people grew up they never learned how to have a good family. It takes a lot of hard work to raise a family. It takes loving sacrifice. Husbands have to lovingly serve their wives. And wives have to lovingly serve their husbands. Well, selfish people don't want to serve anybody. This selfishness has done terrible harm to the family. And the spirit of selfishness is everywhere today.

If you have read stories like those written by Laura Ingalls Wilder, then you know how children grew up in the 1800s. When Almanzo Wilder grew up in New York State as "Farmer Boy", he worked with his father on the farm. Sometimes he went to school, but he learned to be a farmer by working with his father in the fields. In the Bible, you will find that David fed his father's sheep. Rachel fed her father's sheep in the book of Genesis. From the beginning of time, children worked with their father's businesses. But not any more. Since the 1800s, family farms and family businesses have disappeared. Families don't work together much anymore. Most children go off to big school buildings where they are away from their families all day. Dad goes to his workplace, and mom goes to hers. Even when they go to church, often the children go to their classes, and the parents go to their classes. When it comes to their entertainment, everybody gets their own television set. Each member of the family listens to their own music with headphones. Laura Ingalls Wilder didn't have televisions and headphones. Through the long winter evenings, they would sit in the cabin together as a family. They listened to Pa play the violin, and they would sing along with him. Families lived together. They worked together. They danced and sang together. Now these times are gone for most families.

Fixing the Family

We all need to work on making the family stronger. Of course the best place to begin is God's Word. The Bible tells us what fathers, mothers, husbands, and wives are supposed to do. The lessons are simple, but often people do not like to obey them.

Husbands, love your wives. (Colossians 3:19)

Wives, submit to your husbands in the Lord. (Colossians 3:18)

Fathers, bring your children up in the nurture and admonition of the Lord. (Ephesians 6:4)

These are the things that are important to God. Husbands may not love their wives very well, but they need to really work on it. Wives should try to submit to their husbands. Fathers should teach their children God's Word every day. When fathers become so busy that they do not have time to teach their children God's Word, they need to change their schedules. Some people find more time with their children when they homeschool them. Some families will start a home business, so that they can spend more time with their children. There are different ways in which we can make the family strong. But the most important way is for fathers to teach their children from the Bible every day. Some people call this "family worship." This is how we build godly families.

And these words, which I command you this day, shall be in your heart, and you shall teach them diligently to your children, and shall talk of them when you sit in your house, and when you walk by the way, and when you lie down, and when you rise up. And you shall bind them for a sign upon your hand, and they shall be as frontlets between your eyes. And you shall write them on the post of your house, and on your gates.

Deuteronomy 6:6-9

Chapter 6 Review

Ephesians 5:33

Let each one of you in particular so love his own wife as himself, and let the wife see that she respects her husband.

Genesis 2:20-25

So Adam gave names to all cattle, to the birds of the air, and to every beast of the field. But for Adam there was not found a helper comparable to him. And the LORD God caused a deep sleep to fall on Adam, and he slept; and He took one of his ribs, and closed up the flesh in its place. Then the rib which the LORD God had taken from man He made into a woman, and He brought her to the man. And Adam said:

"This is now bone of my bones
And flesh of my flesh;
She shall be called Woman,
Because she was taken out of Man."

Therefore a man shall leave his father and mother and be joined to his wife, and they shall become one flesh. And they were both naked, the man and his wife, and were not ashamed.

1. What is the greatest tragedy of the 20th century according to Dr. James Dobson?

_____

_____

2. While the family in our countries today became very weak, what happened to the state (or government)?

_____

_____

3. What percentage of children in this country are born without fathers now?

_____

What percentage of children in this country were born without fathers in 1960?

_____

4. What is a "Nuclear Family"?

_____

_____

5. What does God say about divorce in Malachi 2:16?

_____

_____

_____

6. How do you get a strong church?

_____

_____

_____

7. What are the four bombs that have destroyed many families?

_____

_____

_____

8. What do we call it when men and women want to enjoy the blessings of marriage together, but they never get married?

_____

9. What do we find Rachel and David (from the Bible) doing when they were children? What was the "farmer boy" Almanzo Wilder doing when he grew up in New York State in the 1800s?

_____

_____

10. How do we make the family stronger? List some of the ways you can make your own family stronger. _____

_____

11. What is "family worship"? _____

_____

12. What are fathers and mothers supposed to do with their children according to Deuteronomy 6:7-9? _____

_____

13. What can you do as a child to make your family stronger? Hint: Read Ephesians 6:1-2.

_____

_____

Vocabulary

Match the word with the correct definition on the right-hand side of the page.

Expense

Researcher

Tragedy

Divorce

Qualifications

Schedule

Submit

Sacrifice

When a husband and/or the wife break up their marriage

A list of the things to do in a day or a week (by time allotments)

An event or events causing great destruction and distress

A quality or accomplishment that makes someone suitable for a particular job or activity

Obeying or yielding to the will of another person

Surrendering your life or something that belongs to you for somebody else

The cost required for something

Somebody who does research about something

What Are Mothers and Fathers Supposed to Do?

Match the appropriate verse to each responsibility.

Verse

1 Timothy 5:8

Titus 2:4

1 Timothy 5:14

Deuteronomy 6:7

Ephesians 5:22

Ephesians 6:4

1 Thessalonians 2:11-12

1 Corinthians 14:35

Titus 2:4

Ephesians 5:25

Titus 2:5

Responsibility

Bring Children Up in Nurture of the Lord

Love Your Children

Love Your Husband

Submit to Husband

Love Your Wife

Encourage, Exhort, and Direct the Children

Work at Home

Manage the Household

Teach God's Word As You Sit in Your House

Teach Your Wife in the Home

Provide Clothing and Food for Wife

Chapter 7

The Church

> ### Matthew 16:18
>
> And I also say to you that you are Peter, and on this rock I will build My church, and the gates of Hades shall not prevail against it.

The Church

Many people believe that the state or civil government is important. Most people still believe that the family is important. But there are so many people that do not see the church as that important. Maybe they think that the church is boring. Maybe they don't see the use of it. Everybody knows that the government is supposed to punish bad guys who rob banks and kill people. The family raises children. But what in the world is the church supposed to do?

Everybody knows the government is supposed to punish bad guys who rob banks and kill people. The family raises children. But what in the world is the church supposed to do?

There are some governments that try to take over the family and the church. They try to do the things that the family is supposed to do and the things that the church is supposed to do. Bad countries have very powerful civil governments that try to take over the responsibilities of the family and the church. As the governments grow more powerful, the families and the churches become weaker. The government makes people think that the church is useless because it is doing what the church is supposed to do.

The Church Is God's Idea

Just like the family is God's idea, the church is God's idea too. Even though many ungodly people today don't like the church, it is very important to God. Picture a husband who really loves his wife very much. She is the most important person in his life. He would give his life for his wife. That's how much he loves her. The church is so important to God that Jesus gave his life for her. This is what we read in Ephesians 5:25:

Husbands, love your wives, just as Christ also loved the church and gave Himself for her.

Ephesians 5:25

108

You can see that the church is very important. It is at least as important as the family.

What Is the Church?

When you think of the church, what do you see in your mind's eye? Is it a building or a group of people? Of course Jesus did not die on the cross for a building made of bricks and wood. Sometimes people meet in buildings, but the building is not a church. It is just a place where people meet. So what is the church? Here is a simple definition:

The Church

The church is a group of people who love each other and gather together to worship the true God in Spirit and in Truth.

John speaks to those people who have fellowship with other believers (1 John 1:3). This is the church. Then John tells us to love the brother whom we can see with our eyes (1 John 4:20). If we cannot love a brother whom we can see, how can we love God Whom we cannot see? A church is a group of people who love God and love each other.

1 John 1:3

That which we have seen and heard we declare to you, that you also may have fellowship with us, and truly, our fellowship is with the Father and with His Son Jesus Christ.

1 John 4:20b

For he who does not love his brother whom he has seen, how can he love God, Whom he has not seen?

These people also gather together to praise God and to fellowship with each other. We find this in the early church in Acts.

So continuing daily with one accord in the temple, and breaking bread from house to house, they ate their food with gladness and simplicity of heart, praising God and having favor with all the people. And the Lord added to the church daily those who were being saved.

Acts 2:46-47

You can see that these people came together with an enthusiastic unity, and they praised God as a group. This is a very simple definition of the church.

What Is the Church Supposed to Do?

Now we need to say a little bit more about the church. Sometimes the church wants to do what the family is supposed to do. Sometimes the government (or the state) wants to do what the church is supposed to do. And sometimes the family tries to do what the church is supposed to do.

If you look in the Bible, you will find that there are several books about the church. One of the most important books is 1 Timothy. In this book, Paul is teaching Timothy how to take care of the church of God (1 Timothy 3:15). We find out several things about the church in this epistle.

1   The church is run by elders. But you can't appoint just anybody to be an elder in the church. He has to meet the qualifications in 1 Timothy 3:1-8.

2   The church is supposed to pay the elders who work really hard to prepare sermons and pray for the people (1 Timothy 5:17).

3   The church is supposed to teach and preach the Word of God to the people (1 Timothy 6:2, 2 Timothy 4:2).

4   The church is also supposed to gather at times to share the Lord's Supper (1 Corinthians 11:18-26).

5   The church takes care of the widows and those in need (1 Timothy 5:8-15).

These are the things the church is supposed to do. Sometimes the church gets very busy doing things it is not supposed to do. And sometimes it forgets to do the things that it is supposed to do. One of the things that most churches don't do very well is taking care of widows. Today, most people just let the government take care of the poor people and the older people.

A widow should be taken care of by her sons and grandsons. If they cannot do it, then the church should take care of her. Notice that it is never the responsibility of the civil government to take care of a widow.

But if you read 1 Timothy 5, you will find that this is the responsibility of the family and the church. If a woman loses her husband, and she cannot afford to pay for food, then who will help her? First, her sons or her grandsons are responsible to take care of her. If they will not take care of her, then they do not belong in the church (1 Timothy 5:8). They have denied the faith. But what if there are no sons or grandsons who are willing to take care of the poor woman? Who should take care of this poor woman so that she doesn't starve to death? Well, many churches believe that the government (or the "state") should take care of her, so they send her to a government office for food and housing. But this is not biblical. The church is supposed to provide for the widow.

The church takes care of the younger widows on an emergency basis. They may get a little help until they can get

111

some work out of the home or until they get married. But the church takes care of the older widows on a full-time basis. These are widows who are over 60 years of age and have served in the church.

Government Welfare and God's Welfare

When poor people get money from the government, they are not thankful. They do not write thank you cards to the government. They begin to think that they deserve these free handouts. The government is stealing money from some people and giving it to others. This is called "socialism." The money they get from the government encourages them not to work. It encourages them to be lazy. When the government gives money to young women who do not have husbands, they do not see a need to get married, so many little boys and girls grow up without fathers. Government welfare is a terrible thing, and it is has ruined many families.

> Socialism is where the government takes money from some people and gives it to others.

God's way of helping poor people is much better. The government is not supposed to give money to poor people. It is the families' and churches' job to help them. When we give money to poor people, we want to make sure that they are not lazy. The church elders or deacons call them every day to make sure that they are working hard. This is how we hold them accountable. We want to make sure they say "thank you" for the help that we give them. Also, we want to see them working to help others in the church too.

It is important that we help the people who we know by name, who live in our local area. When you help somebody in a far-off city, most of the time you do not have a close relationship with them. When we help the poor people, we want it to be voluntary, local, and accountable.

Chapter 7 Review

Matthew 16:18

And I also say to you that you are Peter, and on this rock I will build My church, and the gates of Hades shall not prevail against it.

Acts 2:46-47

So continuing daily with one accord in the temple, and breaking bread from house to house, they ate their food with gladness and simplicity of heart, praising God and having favor with all the people. And the Lord added to the church daily those who were being saved.

1. How did God or Jesus Christ demonstrate His love for the church?

_____

_____

2. What is the simple definition of a church?

_____

_____

_____

3. Who does John tell us to love?

_____

_____

4. Would it be okay if we just watched a video of a church service on television instead of going to church? Why or why not? (Hint: Look up Hebrews 10:25.)

_____

_____

_____

_____

5. According to Acts 2:46-47, what does the church do when it gathers together?

_____

_____

_____

_____

6. How do we treat a fellow who puts in a lot of extra time preparing sermons for the church? (Hint: Look up 1 Timothy 5:17)

7. Which of the following are necessary qualifications for Bishops or Elders (the leaders) who are supposed to lead the church? (Hint: Look up 1 Timothy 3:1-8). Circle the correct answers.

They cannot be addicted to alcohol

They must be very good at mathematics

They must be skilled at teaching

They must have a college degree

They must be rich

They must not be quarrelsome

They must rule their households well

They must be good speakers

They must not love money

They must be gentle

8. Who is responsible for taking care of widows? (Hint: Look up 1 Timothy 5:4, 16)

_____

_____

9. Who are the widows that the church should take care of on a full-time basis?

_____

_____

10. Does the Bible want men or women (or both) teaching and pastoring the church? (Hint: Look up 1 Corinthians 14:34 and 1 Timothy 2:11-12)

_____

11. What does the Bible want men doing in the church according to 1 Timothy 2:8?

_____

_____

_____

What Is a Church Supposed to Do?

Look up the Scripture references on the left side and draw a line
from that reference to the responsibility listed on the right side.

1 Timothy 3:1-8

The church is supposed to pay the elders who work really hard to prepare sermons and pray for the people.

1 Timothy 5:17

The church takes care of the widows and those in need.

1 Timothy 6:2
2 Timothy 4:2

The church is run by elders. But you can't just appoint anybody to be an elder in the church. He has to meet certain qualifications.

1 Corinthians 11:18-26

The church is to gather at times to share the Lord's supper.

1 Timothy 5:8-15

The church is supposed to teach and preach the Word of God to the people.

Vocabulary

Match the word with the correct definition on the right-hand side of the page.

Church

Widow

Elders

Worship

Fellowship

Preach

Lord's Supper

Emergency

Welfare

The expression of reverence and adoration for a deity

To take bread and wine (or grape juice) in communion with Jesus

Leaders of the church

To declare authoritatively the Word of God Himself

A group of people that love each other and worship the true God together

A serious, unexpected, and often dangerous situation requiring immediate action

A woman whose husband has died

Government money to help people with food, clothing, and other necessities and luxuries

A group of people developing unity and demonstrating love by communicating with each other

Chapter 8

The Civil Government

Romans 13:1

Let every soul be subject to the governing authorities. For there is no authority except from God, and the authorities that exist are appointed by God.

118

Civil Government

The first two organizations that God invented were the family and the church. But there is a third organization that God invented for us, and that is civil government.

We do want to know what the Bible says about civil government because the Bible is the Word of God, and God made us. God knows everything about His world. He knows about how it runs, how people act, and how they think. He knows what is best for us, so we should listen to what He has to say. To ignore God's Word would be terribly foolish.

People must learn to live with each other. But this is very difficult to do. This is because men and women are sinful. The Bible says:

The heart is deceitful above all things, and desperately wicked.

Jeremiah 17:9

If everybody was perfect, we would not need civil government. But people often tend to be selfish, lazy, covetous, and even violent. Somehow we must learn to get along with each other on this planet earth. So how do we do this? If we run our families, our churches, and our civil government the way God teaches us in His Word, things will work out pretty well. Sadly, not many people care about what God says. They want to do everything their own way. But if we want a good society with happy families and a happy country, we need to believe God and trust in His Word.

If everybody was perfect, we would not need a civil government. But people like to be selfish, lazy, covetous, and even violent.

What Is Civil Government?

For rulers are not a terror to good works, but to the evil. Will you then not be afraid of the power? Do that which is good, and you shall have praise of the same: for he is the minister of God to you for good. But if you do that which is evil, be afraid; for he bears not the sword in vain: for he is the minister of God, an avenger to execute wrath upon him that does evil.

Romans 13:3-4

This verse speaks very plainly about civil government. We learn two things:

1 People who lead in civil government are ministers of God. Did you know that the President of the United States is a minister, or a servant, of God? All leaders are God's servants. They may not like to admit it. They may get upset if you tell them this. But this is how God looks at them. They may be disobedient servants. They may be bad servants. But they are still God's servants. This is what the Bible tells us. Of course, leaders should try to be good servants. They should learn what the Bible says and obey what it says. In fact, the Word of God instructs kings and rulers to hand-write the Law of God. They must know God's Law from the beginning to the end, and obey it as they rule. This applies to judges, legislators, kings, and presidents.

Leaders should try to be good servants. They should learn what the Bible says and obey what it says.

Also it shall be, when he sits on the throne of his kingdom, that he shall write for himself a copy of this law in a book, from the one before the priests, the Levites. And it shall be with him, and he shall read it all the days of his life, that he may learn to fear the LORD his God and be careful to observe all the words of this law and these statutes, that his heart may not be lifted above his brethren, that he may not turn aside from the commandment to the right hand or to the left, and that he may prolong his days in his kingdom, he and his children in the midst of Israel.

Deuteronomy 17:18-20

2 The second thing we learn from Romans 13 is that the civil government is supposed to "get the bad guys." We use the term "bad guys" for people who steal, and murder people. The Bible calls them "evildoers." But who are these evildoers? What kind of evil do they do? As we said in the fourth chapter, God is the one who decides what is good and what is evil. The ten commandments give us a basic idea of this. So when somebody murders another person, he is breaking the sixth commandment. He has done something evil.

There are two kinds of evildoers. The first evildoer is somebody who comes from another country to kill our people or steal our things. The second kind of evildoer is somebody who is part of our country who kills another citizen. Since there are two kinds of evildoers, there are two parts of government that deal with each one. The department of government that deals with people who attack us from outside of our country is called the Department of Defense. The part of government that deals with the bad guys who come from inside our country is the police department or the judicial branch. In this country, we also have the Federal Bureau of Investigation, Sheriff Departments, and the Marshall's office.

According to Romans 13, evildoers are supposed to fear the government. When good people begin to fear the government, and evil people do not fear the government, you have big problems. This is happening in some of the countries of the world today. If government punishes good people instead of evil people, this is a big problem. Sometimes governments will give free food and shelter to evil people and tax the good people to pay for these things. Why do the evil people fear the government in Romans 13:4? Certainly it is not because the government gives them free food. It is because the government uses the sword to execute wrath. You should understand that the sword will cut and usually will kill. Today the governments use guns instead of swords to kill people. We will look at how the governments use the sword in the next chapter.

Bad Civil Government

There are good civil governments and bad civil governments. Some countries have better governments than others, so it is important for you to understand what makes a good government. When you are older, you must help to build a good government in your country. You should be able to tell the difference between a good government and a bad government.

Bad government destroys families. It takes children away from parents who love them.

Bad government makes it hard for Christians to preach the Gospel and to talk to people about the Bible. This was the sort of government that Peter and the other apostles ran into during the first years of the Christian church. Peter had to remind these evil government officials that they had to obey God rather than men (Acts 5:29).

Acts 5:29

But Peter and the apostles answered, "We must obey God rather than men."

Bad government can put Christians in jail and even kill them. This is happening today in places like North Korea, Vietnam, Iran, and China.

Bad government will allow criminals and mobs to hurt people. It will not stop criminals who steal and kill. Bad government can take away our freedoms and make us its slaves. Is there anything you can do to keep your governments from becoming bad like this? Of course there are ways for you to oppose bad government. But first, you must be able to see the differences between good government and bad government. There are eight mistakes that bad governments make.

1

First, bad civil government takes away freedoms by promising people that it will protect them from poverty. Many people look to government to save them from starvation. So they start to trust in government for this. But when people look to government to save them from poverty, they must give up their freedoms. Government cannot give BOTH security AND freedom. If everybody in this country wants the government to take care of them, then the government will take away all of their freedoms. When this happens, the whole country becomes poor too. So while the government promises that it will take care of the people, it also takes away their freedoms and their wealth!

If people want freedom, they must learn to work hard and take care of their own families. Then we will have good government. If you like freedom, you must not ask the government to take care of your needs—your food, your shelter, your education, and your medical care. If you are afraid of poverty, you must work hard and trust in God. Do not trust in the government. You should trust in God instead! This is what Jesus says in Matthew 6:31-33.

Therefore do not worry, saying, 'What shall we eat?' or 'What shall we drink?' or 'What shall we wear?' For after all these things the Gentiles seek. For your heavenly Father knows that you need all these things. But seek first the kingdom of God and His righteousness, and all these things shall be added to you.

Matthew 6:31-33

Bad civil government discourages people from working. The Bible tells us, "If a man will not work, neither should he eat." If a government is discouraging any person or group of people from working hard six days every week, then it is not a good civil government. People must work to get minerals out of the ground. They must work to turn big chunks of rock into the things we need. They must work to put potato seed into the ground, water the potato plants, dig up the potatoes, and sell them at the market. If everybody is not working hard six days every week, then they will not have food to eat or the other things they need.

Notice that I did not say that civil government should encourage people to work. It is only that government should not discourage people from working. We do not force anybody to work. But most people will work if they are hungry. Working hard is part of the fourth commandment.

A civil government that gives money to people who do not work is a bad government.

Six days you shall labor and do all your work.

Exodus 20:9

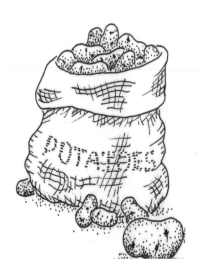

Bad civil government also takes money away from the hardest workers. When people begin to make money, they usually work harder. When you made a little money from washing cars, mowing lawns, or selling something, do you remember how that encouraged you? You saw that your work produced reward.

When people work hard and earn money, a bad civil government looks at the money with greedy eyes. Some people in this government try to get the poor people to covet the money that belongs to the hard-working people. Then these government officials take the money away from them and give part of it to the poor people who will not work.

Suppose that you hired somebody to pull weeds in your garden. He pulled three weeds, and so you gave him 10 candies. Then you hired somebody else, and he pulled 300 weeds out of your garden. So you gave this second fellow 100 candies. Later a government official came and took 60 candies away from the fellow with the 100 candies. He gave 30 candies to the lazy fellow. Of course, the government fellow kept 30 candies for himself too. At the end the lazy fellow had 40 candies, the hard-working fellow had 40 candies, and the government fellow walks away with 30 candies. Do you see that this is wrong? Yet this kind of thing happens in socialist countries all of the time.

When governments encourage poor people to envy rich people, they are encouraging sin. Proverbs 14:30 tells us that envy is the rottenness of the bones. Envy will destroy the happiness of the people and make the country poor. But it is very common today, because of the teaching of Karl Marx. This man taught that governments are supposed to "redistribute the wealth," so that there is nobody in your country who is richer than anybody else. God's Word disagrees with Karl Marx. This is what God's Word says about how the government should tax the poor and the rich:

The rich shall not give more...and the poor shall not give less....You shall do no injustice in judgement. You shall not be partial to the poor, nor honor the person of the mighty.

Exodus 30:15 and Leviticus 19:15

4

Bad civil government also disobeys God's law by lying and stealing. The Bible tells us, "Diverse weights and measures are both alike an abomination to the Lord" (Proverbs 20:10). God does not want anybody changing the value of something without telling others. Suppose you always bought potatoes in a five-pound sack for $5.00. One day you discovered that there were only four pounds of potatoes in the sack. Somebody had removed the weight notation from the label on the sack. But they did not tell you what they had done. Of course, this is dishonest. Well, this is what the government does with our money, all of the time. It changes the value of our money so that it is worth less and less. This is stealing.

5

Bad civil government always tries to take the place of God. When the civil government takes more than 10% in taxes, it is taking more than God asks for in the tithe. In 1 Samuel 8:15-18, the prophet Samuel calls any government that takes more than a tenth of the people's income a "tyranny." Today, the governments that are over us take over 50% of our income. Until about 1913, the American government would not tax its people more than 10%. Since that time, our government has grown into a large tyranny.

He will take a tenth of your grain and your vintage, and give it to his officers and servants. And he will take your male servants, your female servants, your finest young men, and your donkeys, and put them to his work. He will take a tenth of your sheep. And you will be his servants. And you will cry out in that day because of your king whom you have chosen for yourselves, and the LORD will not hear you in that day."

1 Samuel 8:15-18

6

Bad civil government takes away people's property and inheritance. This is what the wicked King Ahab did when he stole Naboth's vineyard. You can read this story in 1 Kings 21:1-10. Eventually the king killed Naboth so he could take his vineyard. It is a terrible thing when governments take away somebody's property (Micah 2:2, Ezekiel 45:9-10).

7

Bad civil government also encourages people to sin against God. A civil government must never lead people to think that sin is okay. It should never tell people that it is okay to kill their unborn babies or to kill very old people. Since 1973, many countries have been doing this sort of thing. These governments should not permit divorce (except in certain cases where the Bible allows it). These governments should never encourage people to skip church on Sundays or discourage people from tithing to the Lord. Certainly, they should never encourage people to break God's Ten Commandments.

8

Finally, bad civil government will punish people who are obeying God. In some countries like Sweden, people are fined for spanking their children. Some children in government schools get in trouble when they pray before eating their lunch. Police in cities like Detroit or Philadelphia have arrested people for preaching God's Word on the streets. These are signs of an evil government.

One of the reasons why we have such a bad government in America is because Christian people do not vote. Many Christians do not know how to vote. They have not read the Bible, so they do not know the difference between a good government and a bad government. Some Christians even believe that God does not want them to get involved in the government.

Chapter 8 Review

Scripture Memory

Romans 13:3-4

For rulers are not a terror to good works, but to the evil. Will you then not be afraid of the power? Do that which is good, and you shall have praise of the same: for he is the minister of God to you for good. But if you do that which is evil, be afraid; for he bears not the sword in vain: for he is the minister of God, a revenger to execute wrath upon him that does evil.

According to the Preamble to the U.S. Constitution (below), what are the six purposes of the federal government?

We the people of the United States, in order to to form a more perfect union, establish justice, insure domestic tranquility, provide for the common defence, promote the general welfare, and secure the blessings of liberty to ourselves and our posterity, do ordain and establish this constitution for the United States of America.

_____

_____

_____

Review Questions

1. What does Paul call the civil ruler in Romans 13:3-4?

_____

2. Why do we need civil governments?

_____

_____

_____

3. What is the civil ruler supposed to do according to Romans 13?

_____

_____

_____

4. What are the two kinds of evildoers?

_____

_____

5. How should evildoers view the government?

_____

_____

6. What are some of the things that bad civil governments do?

_____

_____

_____

7. In what countries around the world do civil governments actually kill Christians or put them in jail?

_____

_____

_____

8. Instead of trusting in government, who should we trust?

_____

9. What did King Ahab do to Naboth?

_____

_____

_____

_____

10. How do bad civil governments encourage people to sin against God?

_____

_____

_____

_____

11. How do bad civil governments punish people for obeying God?

_____

_____

_____

_____

_____

Vocabulary

Match the word with the correct definition on the right-hand side of the page.

Ignore

Civil government

Society

Covetous

Terror

Security

Freedom

Envy

Taxation

Tithe

Tyranny

Property

Inheritance

Extreme fear

The state of being free from danger or threat

Wanting to destroy something that belongs to somebody else

Wanting something that doesn't belong to you

Land and belongings that you give to your children and grandchildren when you die

Buildings and land that belong to somebody

Governments forcing you to pay them money

To refuse to pay attention or to listen to somebody

The 10% of income that needs to go to the church

Very strict, heavy-handed governments

The right to act, speak, or think without control from very strict governments

A group of people who live together in an ordered community

Rulers like judges, presidents, and police officers

Chapter 9
Good Civil Government

Exodus 18:21

Moreover you shall select from all the people able men, such as fear God, men of truth, hating covetousness; and place such over them to be rulers of thousands, rulers of hundreds, rulers of fifties, and rulers of tens.

Good Civil Government

Some governments are better than others. They are a blessing to all that live in those good countries. The Bible describes the difference between bad leaders and good leaders in the following verse:

When the righteous are in authority, the people rejoice; but when a wicked man rules, the people groan.

Proverbs 29:2

But how do we get good government? The Bible gives us three ways to make a good government:

1 First, good government must have good leaders. This should be obvious. It takes good men to make a good government. When the Israelites chose their leaders, Moses told them:

You shall provide out of all the people able men, such as fear God, men of truth, hating covetousness; and place such over them, to be rulers of thousands, and rulers of hundreds, rulers of fifties, and rulers of tens.

Exodus 18:21

There are four basic characteristics listed here for good civil rulers:

Able Men	This means that the men are competent at leading. They can speak well, and they can motivate others to follow them.
Men Who Fear God	This means that these men live every day in the presence of God. They fear God more than they fear men.
Men of Truth	This means that they do not lie.
Men Who Hate Covetousness	This means that they are not motivated by power and money. They are not likely to steal money from the rich to make the government more powerful.

Many of our forefathers would have agreed with this. In fact, the first Chief Justice of the United States Supreme Court, John Jay, wrote:

God has given to our people the choice of their rulers, and it is the duty, as well as the privilege and interest of our Christian nation to select and prefer Christians for our rulers.

If we are going to have good government, we must find righteous leaders who have good character and who lead according to the Word of God. We need leaders who are faithful to their wives, who go to church on Sundays, and who know the Bible inside and out. We cannot waste our time with leaders who hate God and love their sin. Too many of our leaders today reject God's laws, lie to the people, and try to increase the size of the government. They are always trying to get more power.

Good leaders lead justly according to God's standards of justice contained in His law. God's Word has a great deal to say about righteous leadership in government:

How long will you judge unjustly, and show partiality to the wicked? Selah. Defend the poor and fatherless; do justice to the afflicted and needy. Deliver the poor and needy; free them from the hand of the wicked.

Psalm 82:2-4

The God of Israel said, the Rock of Israel spoke to me: "He who rules over men must be just, ruling in the fear of God."

2 Samuel 23:3

The Bible says that leaders must execute justice. This means that the decisions they make and the punishments they bring on crime must be according to what God requires—no more and no less. Our leaders sometimes put parents in jail for spanking their children. This is not justice because God commands parents to discipline their children. Sometimes leaders will let murderers go free. This is not justice either because God's laws require death for murder.

Good leaders must study their Bibles carefully to find out what is just and right. Then the decisions they make will be good decisions. We must go back to the Bible to determine what are good and righteous decisions. If we have good and righteous laws in our country (laws that come from God's Word), then other countries will admire us:

Therefore be careful to observe [God's commands]; for this is your wisdom and your understanding in the sight of the peoples who will hear all these statutes, and say, "Surely this great nation is a wise and understanding people. For what great nation is there that has God so near to it, as the LORD our God is to us, for whatever reason we may call upon Him? And what great nation is there that has such statutes and righteous judgments as are in all this law which I set before you this day?

Deuteronomy 4:6-8

2
The second thing you need to make a good government is good citizens. Romans 13:3 requires us to be good citizens and "do what is good." If we do what is good, righteous leaders will commend us for it.

But as more and more people become lawless, selfish, and destructive, the government will become harder on everybody. This is how wicked governments get more power. When neighbors fight with each other, they ask the government to fix their problems. Every time they do this, they make the government more powerful. Every time men sue each other or steal things from each other, they make governments more powerful.

We must do what is good. We must govern ourselves according to God's laws. We must take care of our own poor people instead of turning them over to the government. God has commanded that we take care of the poor as the Good Samaritan helped the wounded man on the road. The good man did not turn the man over to a government agency. He took care of the poor man by himself. God tells us to tithe 10% of our money to the church. Sadly, Christians in America give only 2%, on average, to the church. So the government taxes them over 50% of their income (five times what it should be). If Christians would only obey God's Word and be generous to the poor and to the church, they would not live in a tyranny! You must be a generous man if you will be free.

> God has commanded that we take care of the poor as the Good Samaritan helped the wounded man on the road.

God has also commanded that we take care of our parents when they are old if they need help. We should not expect the government to take care of them. Jesus was upset with the Pharisees who stopped taking care of their parents in their old age (see Matthew 15:1-8). Is Jesus upset with Americans who do not take care of their parents in their old age?

As we mentioned in Chapter 6, it is the parents' responsibility to take care of the education of their children. If we send them to government schools and have the government pay for their education, we are giving up our responsibility. When we are lazy, irresponsible, and immoral, we will see governments grow in power. But we will have good government if we govern ourselves well.

There is one more thing that you need if you will have good government. We will address this in the next chapter.

Chapter 9 Review

Scripture Memory

Exodus 18:21

Moreover you shall select from all the people able men, such as fear God, men of truth, hating covetousness; and place such over them to be rulers of thousands, rulers of hundreds, rulers of fifties, and rulers of tens.

Scripture Reading

2 Thessalonians 3:10

For even when we were with you, we commanded you this: if anyone will not work, neither shall he eat.

Proverbs 14:4

Where no oxen are, the trough is clean; but much increase comes by the strength of an ox.

Proverbs 16:2

All the ways of a man are pure in his own eyes, but the Lord weighs the spirits.

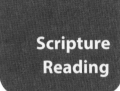

Scripture Reading

Proverbs 21:3

To do righteousness and justice is more acceptable to the Lord than sacrifice.

Micah 6:8

He has shown you, O man, what is good; and what does the Lord require of you but to do justly, to love mercy, and to walk humbly with your God?

1. Give several examples of countries that have had better governments over the last hundred years. Give several examples of countries that have had bad governments.

_____

_____

2. When the righteous are in authority, what do the people do?

_____

3. When the wicked rule, what do the people do?

_____

_____

4. According to Exodus 18:21 what are the basic requirements for good leaders?

_____

_____

5. Which commandment tells us to work hard six days a week?

_____

_____

6. What are the three things you need in order to get good government?

_____

_____

7. What happens to the civil government when the people become lawless, selfish, and destructive?

_____

_____

8. What did the Good Samaritan do for the poor and wounded man on the side of the road? Did he call the government to get involved?

_____

_____

_____

9. How can good leaders find out what is a just and right thing to do?

_____

_____

_____

The Three Spheres of Government

Choose which sphere of government should be responsible for the following duties. Whose job is it to do the following? Is it the civil government's job? Is it the church's job? Is it your families job?

_____ appointing pastors

_____ feeding and clothing children

_____ capturing criminals

_____ supporting poor widows and orphans

_____ disciplining children

_____ sending missionaries to other countries to preach the gospel

_____ deciding if a teenager is old enough to hunt

_____ defending our nation from terrorists

_____ deciding which school children should attend

_____ baptizing people

_____ collecting tithes and offerings and spending that money

_____ defending our nation's borders from invasion

_____ prosecuting criminals and collecting taxes

_____ taking care of grandparents when they need care

Vocabulary

Match the word with the correct definition on the right-hand side of the page.

Competent

Characteristic

Standards

Justice

Motivated

Citizen

Judicial

Legislature

Privilege

Irresponsible

Immoral

A feature or quality belonging typically to a person, place, or thing and serving to identify it

An inhabitant of a particular city or nation

Breaking God's laws

A required level of morality or quality

What is right (according to God's law)

The part of a civil magistrate that makes the laws

Not fulfilling your duties and responsibilities

The part of a civil magistrate that decides if you've broken the law

Able to perform a task

Excited about doing something

A special right or advantage

10 Good Law

" Micah 6:8

He has shown you, O man, what is good; and what does the LORD require of you but to do justly, to love mercy, and to walk humbly with your God?

Good Law

You should remember there are three things that make for good government. In the last chapter, we talked about good leaders and good citizens. Without good citizens, even good leaders might be pressed to turn the country into a tyranny. You might even find a society with upright citizens ruled by an evil dictator. For good government you need three things: good leaders, good citizens, and good laws.

3 The third thing required for good government is good law. Both the citizens and the leaders must be able to tell the difference between good laws and bad laws.

Governments must write their laws somewhere so that everybody knows the laws they must obey. There must not be any confusion about these laws. We need to know the laws that the government expects us to obey. The same thing applies to your family. You need to know the rules in the home that your dad and mom expect you to obey.

For good government, you need three things: good leaders, good citizens, and good laws.

There are two parts of civil government. The legislature is supposed to let us know what laws they want us to obey. Then the judges and the police are supposed to enforce these laws. That means that if somebody breaks the law, it is the judges who will make sure that he will pay the penalty for breaking the law. What if there was a law against brushing your sister's hair? Of course, there is nothing wrong with brushing your sister's hair. In fact, this is a nice thing to do. If the police arrested you for brushing your sister's hair and put you in prison for it, we would call that a bad law. To have a good civil government, you need a government that makes good laws and doesn't make bad laws. Where there are bad laws, there are bad governments and evil countries. A country with good laws will be a really nice place to live.

What Is a Good Law?

Now I hope that you can see how important it is for governments to use good laws. But this takes us back to a question we asked earlier in this study guide: "What is right and wrong?" Almost everybody has an opinion on what is right and what is wrong. There are many ways to decide what kind of laws we need to make in government. Sometimes people who run the government will take an opinion poll and ask people what they think. If most people think that killing unborn babies is a good idea, then these leaders will decide that abortion should be legal. But this is not a good way to make good laws. People change their minds all of the time. Besides, you cannot depend on sinful and ignorant people to make the right decisions. Sometimes when we make laws this way, we can make a mistake and make a bad law. What do you think is the very best way to decide what good laws are?

> If most people think that killing unborn babies is a good idea, then some leaders will decide that abortion should be legal. But this is not a good way to make good laws.

Since God made the world, and He gave us the Bible for answers for everything, then it seems that we have a very important book to help us choose good laws. Most Christians agree that the Bible has some good things to say about how we should behave in our own lives. But not everybody uses the Bible to decide what laws to make in civil government.

We know that the Bible has a lot to say about everything—even the civil government. The Puritans and Pilgrims who founded America believed this. They used the Bible to make good laws when they set up a government in the 1600s. Many people believe that is why God has blessed America so much.

For something as important as government, we know God wouldn't have left us without any idea of right and wrong. In the Bible, God tells us to be righteous and do justice in the courts (Micah 6:8, Isaiah 1:17, and 2 Samuel 23:3). This is especially important for our government leaders. They need to know which are the right decisions to make and which are the right laws to use.

Learn to do good;
Seek justice,
Rebuke the oppressor;
Defend the fatherless,
Plead for the widow.
Isaiah 1:17

All of us should look to the Bible first to decide what is just and right. Everybody who votes, the people who make laws, and the people who judge must all know what the Bible says about what is right and wrong. All should read the Bible with a humble spirit and ask God, "What do you want me to learn from You in Your Holy Word?"

The Most Important Law

We will now take a look at a few laws in the Bible. We do not have enough room in this study to talk about all of the laws in the Bible. As you grow older, you will need to study all of the laws in the Old and New Testaments. Remember that all of Scripture is given to prepare you for every good work (2 Timothy 3:16-17). If you are going to vote someday, or if you are going to be a leader in government, you will need to know God's laws. That will prepare you to vote righteously.

We will begin with the most important law of all. It is repeated more than any other civil law in the Bible. God is very clear when He communicates to us. There is no question about what He means. God wants capital punishment for murder. This means that God wants the government to put the murderer to death. This law is so important that it was the first law God gave to Noah after the Flood:

"Whoever sheds man's blood, by man his blood shall be shed; for in the image of God He made man" (Genesis 9:6).

This is the first mention of government and civil penalties in the Bible. There was no mention of it before the Flood. Way back then, men became very bad to the point that God had to destroy the whole world. So now God gives Noah one law for civil government. God wants men to get along with each other. This law will keep people safe in their societies until He gives them more laws later on. It is only ONE LAW, but it is the most basic law that God has given for human government. God never changed His mind on this law anywhere in the Bible. Even Paul reminds us that the government uses the sword against the evildoers in Romans 13. We must not question God's wisdom or His justice. God is completely just, and He gives us His truth. He knows what is best for us. It may not be pleasant to consider putting somebody to death, but we are not God. We must not suggest that God is unjust. The government must put the murderer to death.

But what is this shedding of blood? What is murder? First of all, murder is not killing somebody by accident. From time to time, somebody swings an ax and the head flies off and kills somebody. This is an accident. Sometimes people also kill in self-defense. The Bible allows us to defend ourselves and others from somebody who is trying to kill us (Exodus 22:2-3). Murder is beating a person to death in a fit of anger (Exodus 21:20). The Bible also defines the murderer as somebody who was planning to kill somebody by "lying in wait." Also, there must be hate in the heart

148

(see Exodus 21:14, 28-30, Numbers 35:22-23, and Deuteronomy 19:4-6, 11-16). Today we call this "forethought and malice."

Restitution

God also forbids stealing. This means that people must own things. When somebody owns something, it is wrong for another person to take it away from him. But what should the government do when people steal things from other people?

God is very wise in these matters, much wiser than men. He requires restitution. Most governments in today's world disagree with this. When thieves are caught, they are sent to places called "prisons." In these places, the thieves live with other criminals where they pick up more bad habits. The government requires the hardworking citizens to pay for the prisons so that thieves can have warm beds, good food, and doctors to take care of them. The victims of the crimes have to pay taxes to keep these prisons. Of course, this is not just and right. That is why the Bible does not want us to have prisons.

Instead of prisons, the Bible requires "restitution." This does not mean that criminals should pay the government when they break the law. This means that they should pay their VICTIMS when they steal money from them. This is a wonderful system of justice because it is God's system. Here are some examples of how this system works.

When a robber steals something from you but returns what he stole undamaged, then he must pay you back twice the value (Exodus 22:4). For example, if a robber stole your father's car that was worth $4,000, he would have to pay another $4,000 to your father even after returning the car undamaged.

But if the robber does not have the stolen goods in his possession any more, then he must pay back four times its value (Exodus 22:1). If the robber stole your Laborador Retriever puppy that you bought for $200, and then sold it to somebody else, he would have to pay you $800 in a court of law.

If a robber turns himself in and confesses to the crime, then he has to return what he has stolen and pay you 20% of the value. Suppose for example that a robber breaks into your house and steals your stamp collection that is worth $100. If he starts to feel guilty about it and confesses to the crime, then he must return your stamp collection and pay you $20.

If somebody ruins another person's property on purpose, he or she must pay for the damage (Exodus 22:6). For example, if a vandal breaks a window in your house and spray paints nasty words on the outside walls, then he must pay for a new window and a new paint job on the house.

But what happens if the criminals do not have any money to pay the restitution to their victims? Then, the Bible has a simple solution to this. They must work for the victim until the debt is paid (Exodus 22:3). If they refuse to work to pay the restitution, then they must be put to death (see Deuteronomy 17:8-13). You can see how this is a very good system of law. It may seem a little bit strict, but that is because it is just and right. We must never argue with God's justice because God is much wiser than us. He is completely and absolutely just.

These are only a few examples of good laws. There are also many other good laws in the Bible. We know that they are good laws because God wrote them, and He is holy, just, and good.

The Bible has a lot to say about good leaders, good citizens, and good laws. If you want to have a good country, then you need to obey God's laws. This is the simple message of Deuteronomy 28.

"Now it shall come to pass, if you diligently obey the voice of the LORD your God, to observe carefully all His commandments which I command you today, that the LORD your God will set you high above all nations of the earth. And all these blessings shall come upon you and overtake you, because you obey the voice of the LORD your God: blessed shall you be in the city, and blessed shall you be in the country" (Deuteronomy 28:1-3).

Witnesses in Court

How do you know that somebody is guilty of a crime? When the police find the body of a man who has been murdered, they begin to look for the guy who did it. Often, it is difficult to find the murderer because he tries to cover his tracks. He does not want the police to find him. When the police find somebody whom they think did the crime, they call him "the suspect." The judge and the jury (citizen judges) must figure out whether or not he did the crime.

The Bible has very important rules about witnesses. The most important rule is that there must be at least two or three witnesses to establish the truth of a crime. You cannot rely on one witness. This means that some crimes will go unpunished by human courts. But we know that God is the wise Judge over all things, and God will deal justly with the man who did the crimes.

One witness shall not rise against a man concerning any iniquity or any sin that he commits; by the mouth of two or three witnesses the matter shall be established.

Deuteronomy 19:15

More Things You Need to Know About Government

There are many other issues relating to government that you will study as you grow older. The important thing is to ask the question, "What does the Bible say about that?" Then, you look through the Bible to get some idea of what God says about these things. For now, we will consider just a few other governmental issues.

Taxation

Government should not take everybody's money away from them. God only asks for a tenth of our money for our tithe at church, so government should not take more than one-tenth of the money that we earn.

"And [the king] will take a tenth of your grain, and your vintage...and you will cry out in that day because of your king whom you have chosen for yourselves, and the Lord will not hear you in that day" (1 Samuel 8:15-18).

Our governments in this country take between 50% and 60% of what the people earn now. This is far more than what God prescribed in the Bible. The government is stealing money when it takes more than it is supposed to take. If we want a free country, then the government must stop taking so much money from the people.

The civil government should not tax inheritance or people's houses. The government also should not try to take away people's property. King Ahab took Naboth's vineyard away from him, and God condemned him for that (1 Kings 21:3, Proverbs 13:22). The civil government should not take peoples' homes away from them to pay for taxes. The Bible says that peoples' property is sacred and it is an abomination to God when the property markers are moved. This is why property taxes are bad too (Deuteronomy 19:14, 27:17, Proverbs 22:28).

Everybody should pay the same in taxes. The civil government should not make some people pay more than others. That is unfair. The Bible says that the government should treat the poor and the rich just the same.

"You shall do no unrighteousness in judgment: you shall not respect the person of the poor, nor honor the person of the mighty: but in righteousness shall you judge your neighbor" (Leviticus 19:15).

Government Debt

Government should not go into debt to pay its bills. People who spend more money than they get should not be leaders in government. The Bible says that debt is bad, especially if we want to have a strong and healthy country (Romans 13:8, Proverbs 22:7). The way that government should get out of debt is to stop spending so much money. Our government should not raise our taxes. It should stop spending so much money and decrease our taxes.

Government Rules and Regulations

"Because of the transgression of the land many are its princes; but by a man of understanding and knowledge right will be prolonged." (Proverbs 28:2)

People can do what they want with their own property, but they should never hurt the property of others. The government should not punish people by collecting fines from them and keeping those fines for itself. Government should make somebody who did damage to some person's property pay back the person who was hurt.

If a lot of people are hurt when they use a product made by some company, then those people who made the product should help pay for the medical bills. The government shouldn't create all kinds of rules and regulations telling people how to make things and what labels to put on those things. But the companies should understand that they may have to pay if the things that they make hurt people.

 **Money**

"Diverse weights and diverse measures, They are alike, an abomination to the Lord." (Proverbs 20:10)

A bank called the Federal Reserve controls the amount of money in our economy. Whenever it wants to, it prints lots of money and pretends to lend it to the government. The government steals from the people by taking all of this new printed money from the Federal Reserve. This is called artificial inflation. When the Federal Reserve prints this money, it devalues people's money. It secretly adjusts the value of our money that we use to buy things. The Book of Proverbs calls this behavior an "abomination to God."

 **Foreign Policy**

How a Country Should Get Along with Other Countries

"When a man's ways please the LORD, He makes even his enemies to be at peace with him." (Proverbs 16:7)

No government of men should try to rule the whole world. Only God should rule the world. Just as God wouldn't let the people of Babel get too big and powerful, we should not let any government get too big and powerful.

Our government also should never borrow money from other countries (Deuteronomy 15:6, 28:12).

Our government should never just give away our money to other countries. If we want to give money to poor people or missionaries in other countries then we will give our own money away. The government shouldn't take our money away from us and give it away to evil countries around the world.

As much as is possible, our government should keep its nose out of the business of other countries, especially when the countries are fighting wars. The purpose of our government is to defend us from bad people who might invade our country or do criminal things here in our country. The best way to make peace in other countries is to send missionaries there to teach them how to love each other as Christ loved us. Our government should do everything possible to protect our missionaries in other countries.

Defense

According to the Bible the purpose of civil government is to "bear the sword" against evildoers (Romans 13:3). Some of those evildoers come from other countries to attack us and enslave our people. That's why every government must have a good system of defense.

When we fight wars, we should be careful not to kill innocent women and children. The Bible says we should only kill the fighting men (Deuteronomy 20:13-14).

Crime

The government is supposed to punish people who commit crimes. This punishment should be restitution or capital punishment.

Crime is getting worse and worse in America. So instead of obeying the Bible, our government builds more prisons and gives the prisoners better food, education, and medical treatment. The government should not try to take care of crime by getting more police and more investigations into people's houses and things. This is foolish. Instead, the government should start using God's methods of punishment, like restitution and capital punishment.

Those who are found guilty of capital crimes should be put to death (Genesis 9:6, Acts 25:11). Those who steal should make restitution to their victims (Exodus 22:1,4). If the thief cannot pay his victims back, then he must work until it is paid off.

There must be more than one witness to convict a person of a crime. The Bible requires two or three witnesses. Anybody who tells a lie in court against somebody who is on trial should be punished. In fact, the Bible says that the person who lies in court should receive the punishment that the person who was on trial would have received (Deuteronomy 17:5, 19:5, 16-21).

Family

Government officials should never be allowed into our houses without a warrant written by a judge (Proverbs 23:10).

Parents should be able to teach, train, and discipline their children without the government interrupting them.

God has put parents in charge of children (Deuteronomy 6:1-12, Ephesians 6:1 4). So parents should decide what their children should eat, what their children should learn, when their children get their shots, and how their children should spend their time.

Abortion

We are very sad because many American parents kill their little babies before they are born. We know that the government wants people to kill their children because it gives away our tax money to baby-killing businesses like *Planned Parenthood*. Americans have killed almost 55 million babies over the last 38 years. God judges nations when they shed innocent blood (Jeremiah 22:3-17, Isaiah 1:14-16, Exodus 22:22-24).

The Bible is against murder whether it is commited against a little baby, an old man, a rich person, or a poor person. We must stop all of this murder. The government must make laws against abortion. The government should never give money to people who commit this crime.

⇨ Euthanasia

Some doctors and politicians who support baby killing also would like to start killing older people. This is also against God's laws. Since governments are running out of money to take care of old people, it is very possible they will try to kill the older sick ones.

⇨ Schools

"And you shall teach my words diligently to your children, and shall talk of them when you sit up in your house, when you walk by the way, when you lie down, and when you rise up" (Deuteronomy 6:7).

In the Bible, God puts parents and churches in charge of teaching people. Big and powerful government officials like to pay for education because they want everybody to keep voting for big government. So they train children when they are very young to depend on and appreciate big government.

The civil government should not tell parents what kind of textbooks they can use or what kind of test they should give to their children. The government should never force children to take certain tests. Neither should government officials have to see our school records or snoop around our homes to see when the children are in school and when they're not in school. This is not the government's business.

Churches and private organizations should provide schools for poor children who need an education (if necessary). The government is not being kind to poor people when they steal money from other people to pay for education. Government schools train families and children to be dependent on the government for everything.

➡ Guns

"Then He said to them, "But now, he who has a money bag, let him take it, and likewise a knapsack; and he who has no sword, let him sell his garment and buy one." (Luke 22:36).

Jesus told his disciples to buy swords so they could protect themselves. This is because self-defense is a very important right that we should never give away to government. People should be able to buy guns and use them to protect themselves.

The civil government should never take away guns from people who are law-abiding citizens. America's Bill of Rights tells us that government should not "infringe on" our right to carry and own guns. This means that the government should not even be trying to keep track of the names of people who own guns.

Chapter 10 Review

Scripture Memory

Romans 7:12

Therefore the law is holy, and the commandment holy and just and good.

John 14:15

If you love Me, keep My commandments.

1 John 2:4

He who says, 'I know Him,' and does not keep His commandments is a liar, and the truth is not in him.

Scripture Reading

Psalm 1

Blessed is the man who walks not in the counsel of the ungodly, nor stands in the path of sinners, nor sits in the seat of the scornful; but his delight is in the law of the LORD, and in His law he meditates day and night.
He shall be like a tree planted by the rivers of water, that brings forth its fruit in its season, whose leaf also shall not wither; and whatever he does shall prosper. The ungodly are not so, but are like the chaff which the wind drives away. Therefore the ungodly shall not stand in the judgment, nor sinners in the congregation of the righteous. For the LORD knows the way of the righteous, but the way of the ungodly shall perish.

1. What are the two basic parts of a civil government?

_____

_____

2. How do you know that a civil law is a good law?

_____

3. What is the most basic civil law of all?

_____

_____

4. Where is the first civil law mentioned in the Bible?

_____

_____

5. What is self-defense?

_____

_____

6. Read Numbers 35:11. What should happen to somebody who accidentally kills somebody else?

_____

_____

7. What is the problem with prisons?

_____

_____

8. Describe restitution (in your own words).

_____

_____

9. What should happen to the fellow who steals your bicycle (according to biblical law)?

_____

_____

_____

10. What happens if the criminals do not have enough money to pay the victims what they have stolen?

_____

_____

_____

11. How many witnesses does it take to prove a case in a criminal trial (according to the Bible)?

_____

12. According to 1 Samuel 8:15-18, what is the most a government should ever tax its people?

_____

13. What did Jesus say about swords and weapons of defense?

_____

Vocabulary

Match the word with the correct definition on the right-hand side of the page.

Words	Definitions
Dictator	Killing children in their mothers' wombs
Penalty	Returning to the victim the things you have stolen (and usually a little extra)
Legal	Planning ahead of time what you will do
Illegal	When the state puts somebody to death (by shooting, hanging, or electrical shock)
Capital Punishment	In accordance with the law of the country or state
Forethought	Evil intent and hatred in your heart
Malice	Against the law of the country or state
Restitution	A punishment for a crime committed (when somebody does something bad)
Abomination	Killing the older people in our society
Foreign Policy	How we get along with foreign countries
Abortion	A tyrant, a very harsh political ruler with too much power
Euthanasia	Something very horrible or appalling

Answer Key

Chapter 1
1. The biggest lie people tell is that there is no God.
2. The beginning of wisdom and knowledge is the fear of the Lord (Proverbs 1:7).
3. It would be very dangerous.
4. I can trust God completely because he knows all things while men do not know all things.
5. God created everything.
6. He told Adam not to eat from the tree of the knowledge of good and evil.
7. We are sinners and we need to know God's Word.
8. We find God's truth in the Holy Bible.
9. Answers may include: Adam, Noah, Abraham, Moses, David, John the Baptist, The Apostles.
10. The Bible is to equip us for every good work.
11. Yes, we can use the Bible in all areas of life.
12. The Bible is trustworthy because it is God's Word.
13. The use of glasses to see things in the world.
14. To see if someone has a biblical worldview, we can ask what he thinks about any subject and see whether he starts with the Bible.
15. They will have their place in the lake which burns with fire and brimstone.
16: What Does the Bible Say About That?
17: You should believe God's Word
18: Where You There?
19: God formed man out of the dust of the ground, and breathed the breath of life into him.

Vocabulary
Truth - That which is true or in accordance with fact or reality

Significant - Important

Dangerous - Able or likely to cause harm or injury

Ignorant - Stupid or uninformed

Relationship - The way in which two people are connected

Instructions - A direction or order

Cultivate - Prepare or use land for sowing or planting

Opinion - A view or judgment formed about something, not necessarily based on fact or knowledge

Authority - The power or right to give orders, make decisions, and enforce obedience

Trustworthy - Able to be relied on as honest or truthful

Worldview - A particular philosophy of life or conception of the world

Confident - Feeling or showing certainty about something

Fossils - The remains or impression of a creature preserved in petrified form or as a mold or cast in rock

Chapter 2
1. Cars and houses come from God.
2. God made the materials necessary for cars and houses.
3. It would explode and move the sand but it would not create anything.
4. God created the very first plants and animals on the third and fifth day of creation.
5. God created the first man on the sixth day of creation.
6. Volcanoes erupt by God's direction.
7. Mount St. Helens.
8. The Global Flood.

9. God intended to kill all plants, animals, and people on the earth.

10. Concepts like "love."

11. God is a Spirit.

12. We know that God is real because the Holy Bible tells us so.

13. God tells us that light, man, plants, and birds are all real. If the Bible tells us that they are real, then they are real.

14. It means that He is in control of everything that happens.

15. God knows what you will roll (Proverbs 16:33). He directs the roll of the dice and knows all things.

16. God made him look and act like a beast to humble him.

17. Humanism is the attempt of man to be in control of all things.

18. Men make their governments big and powerful so that they can control the future.

Vocabulary

Universities - Schools offering advanced teaching (after you graduate from high school)

Evolved - Develop gradually, esp. from a simple to a more complex form

Accident - An incident that happens by chance (nothing causes it)

Creation - The action or process of bringing something into existence

Providence - The work of God caring for his creation

Preserving - Maintain (something) in its original or existing state

Governing - Ruling

Philosophers - A person engaged or learned in philosophy, esp. as an academic discipline

Revelation - The making known of a secret or the unknown

Reality - The world or the state of things as they actually exist

Sovereign - Possessing supreme or ultimate power

Vote - Choosing somebody to rule over you

Election - The process of electing people to rule over you

Certainty - The quality of being reliably true

Chapter 3

1. "Does God exist?" is a bigger question.

2. Worldview is a collection of answers to the big questions.

3. Epistemology, Metaphysics, and Ethics.

4. Catching a Cold – E

Stealing a Candy Bar – W

Lying to Your Parents – W

Tripping on a big rock and skinning your knee – E

Falling in a river and drowning – E

Throwing a rock in anger at your brother – W

Accidently riding your bike into your friend – E

Hitting a ball into your neighbor's glass door – W

5. The conscience makes us feel bad and guilty.

6. Men who have seared consciences don't feel as bad when they do bad things.

7. Adam was created good, and he always did the right thing.

8. He disobeyed God by eating of the forbidden tree.

9. The only way we can figure out what is right and wrong and good and evil is to see what God's Word says.

10. If you try to do things that make you happy all the time you may sin against others and hurt them.

11. Ten Commandments.

12. The Fifth Commandment.

13. We are to love God and our neighbor.

14. We love God and our neighbor by keeping God's commandments.

15. 1 Timothy 5:17-18.

16. You should build a fence around the roof so that no one falls off and gets hurt.

17. Boys should not wear girls' clothes, and girls should not wear boys' clothes.

18. The third and ninth commandments. The third commandment forbids us to take the Lord's name in vain. The ninth commandment forbids us to bear false witness against our neighbor.
19. Babies in the womb are created and formed by God.

Cross Word Puzzle
Ethics - The study of moral principles, right and wrong
Absolute - A value or principle that is always true or right
Conscience - The part of us that is sensitive to right and wrong
Seared - Dried up or withered
Metaphysics - The study of reality
Epistemology - The study of truth
Determine - To firmly decide
Abortion - Killing a child in its mother's womb

Chapter 4
1. Genesis 2:18.
2. Body and Spirit.
3. Answers may vary: God is sovereign, while man is not. God creates things, but man does not.
4. Answers may vary: Man can think, love, and communicate.
5. Animals do not feel guilt. Man feels guilt because he is a moral creature.
6. The big problem is sin.
7. Lack of money and ignorance.
8. The wages of sin is death.
9. Station #1 – Man is without sin
Station #2 – Man is dead in sin and will die in sin and suffer eternal death.
Station #3 – Through the gospel men are saved from their sins.
Station #4 – Man is perfected and is free from sin and death.
10. Answers may vary.
11. Sin is the breaking of God's law.
12. The heart which is corrupt and evil.
13. Jesus Christ is the Son of God who is Lord and Savior.
14. Jesus came to earth to save his people from their sins.
15. Answers may vary: We are sanctified and become more holy. Our guilt is removed. He improves our relationships with our parents.

Vocabulary
Anthropology - The study of you (or the study of man)
Sociology - The study of your relationship with other people in the world
Disappoint - To fail to fulfill the hopes or expectations of (someone)
Guilt - The feeling you get when you have done something bad
Characteristic - A feature or quality belonging typically to a person, place, or thing
Accountable - Being responsible to obey somebody
Poverty - The state of being poor
Influence - Tempting or encouraging a person to do something (good or bad)
Advanced - Higher levels of complexity
Species - A type of animal or mammal
Image - A representation of something or somebody else
Disrupt - To interrupt by causing a disturbance or a problem
Obvious - Easily perceived or understood
Invisible - Without physical form and impossible to see with the eyes
Similarities - The state of being similar or sharing the same characteristics
Consequences - The results of an action, sometimes a punishment for an action

Sanctification - Moral improvement, becoming holy

Chapter 5

1. The people in charge of the family are the father and mother.
2. The people in the charge of the church are pastors and elders.
3. The people in the charge of the state are presidents, governors, senators, and judges.
4. The state.
5. God.
6. The father (Proverbs 13:24).
7. The father does not have the responsibility or authority to shoot bad guys; it is the job of the state.
8. The state did not have the authority to throw John Bunyan into jail for preaching.
9. Families
10. The church and family will be destroyed.
11. Marxists or Socialists.
12. He was trying to get rid of the family and increase the size of the state.

Vocabulary

Community - A group of people living together, in relationship with each other
Organizations - A group of people
Essential - Vitally important, very important
Undisciplined - Not behaving well, disorderly
Government - An authority established by God that governs or rules
Regulations - Rules
Interfere - Getting in the way, trying to rule over something illegitimately
Socialists - People who empower the state to solve all their problems for them
Church - A body of people from different families that gather to hear God's Word and worship God together
Family - A father, mother, and children (as God provides)

Chapter 6

1. The breakdown of the family in the West.
2. The government has grown very powerful.
3. 41% of children in 2009, 6% of children in 1960.
4. The nuclear family consists of a dad, mom, and children.
5. God hates divorce.
6. Good strong families are necessary to have a strong church.
7. The government bomb, the fornication bomb, the "it's all about me" bomb, and the family splitting bomb.
8. Fornication.
9. The children worked with their parents.
10. Answers may vary: Husbands should love their wives. Wives should submit to their husbands. Children should obey their parents.
11. Family worship is the practice of learning God's Word together as a family.
12. The father and mother are to teach their children the Word of God.
13. Honor and obey my parents.

Vocabulary

Expense - The cost required for something
Researcher - Somebody who does research about something
Tragedy - An event or events causing great destruction and distress
Divorce - When a husband and/or the wife break up their marriage
Qualifications - A quality or accomplishment that makes someone suitable for a particular job or activity
Schedule - A list of the things to do in a day or a week (by time allotments)
Submit - Obeying or yielding to the will of another person
Sacrifice - Surrendering your life or something that belongs to you for somebody else

Chapter 7

1. Jesus died for the church.
2. The church is a group of people who love each other and gather together to worship the true God in Spirit and in Truth.
3. We are told to love our brother.
4. We are commanded to gather together.
5. The church broke bread and gave thanks and praise to God.
6. We are to pay him for his work and give him the double honor.
7. They cannot be addicted to alcohol, they must be skilled at teaching, they must not be quarrelsome, they must rule their households well, they must not love money, they must be gentle.
8. Sons and grandsons.
9. Those who are 60 or older, have been the wife of one man, trust in God, are well reported for good works, and are not taken care of by their family (see 1 Timothy 5).
10. The Bible teaches that men should teach and pastor in the church.
11. Men are to pray, lifting hands, without quarreling or wrath.

"What is the church supposed to do?" Activity

1 Timothy 3:1-8 – The church is run by elders. But you can't just appoint anybody to be an elder in the church. They have to meet certain qualifications.

1 Timothy 5:17 – The church is supposed to pay the elders who work really hard to prepare sermons and to pray for the people.

1 Timothy 6:2; 2 Timothy 4:2 – The church is supposed to teach and preach the word of God to the people.

1 Corinthians 11:18-24 – The church is to gather at times to share the Lord's Supper.

1 Timothy 5:8-15 – The church takes care of the widows and those in need.

Vocabulary
Church - A group of people that love each other and worship the true God together
Widow - A woman whose husband has died
Elders - Leaders of the church
Worship - The expression of reverence and adoration for a deity
Fellowship - A group of people developing unity and demonstrating love by communicating with each other
Preach - To declare authoritatively the Word of God
Lord's Supper - To take bread and wine or grape juice in communion with Jesus
Emergency - A serious, unexpected, and often dangerous situation requiring immediate action
Welfare - Government money to help people with food, clothing, and other necessities and luxuries

Chapter 8
Constitution Activity:
Form a more perfect union, establish justice, insure domestic tranquility, provide for the common defense, promote the general welfare, secure the blessings of liberty for us and our posterity.

1. God's minister for good.
2. To keep order in society and enforce God's law.
3. Punish evil and reward good.
4. The first kind of evildoer comes into the country to do harm. The second kind of evildoer is a citizen of the country.
5. Evildoers should fear the government.

6. Answers may vary: Bad governments destroy families, make the Gospel hard to preach, and do not punish criminals.

7. Answers may vary: North Korea, China, Vietnam, Iran.

8. We should trust in God.

9. He murdered Naboth and took his property.

10. They permit the breaking of God's law.

11. They will punish and fine people who seek to obey God's law.

Vocabulary

Ignore – To refuse to pay attention or listen to somebody

Civil Government – Rulers like judges, presidents, and police officers

Society – A group of people who live together in an ordered community

Covetous – Wanting something that doesn't belong to you

Terror – Extreme fear

Security – The state of being free from danger or threat

Freedom - The right to act, speak, or think, without control from very strict governments

Envy – Wanting to destroy something that belongs to somebody else

Taxation – Governments forcing you to pay them money

Tithe – The 10% of income that needs to go to the church

Tyranny – Very strict, heavy-handed governments

Property – Buildings and land that belong to somebody

Inheritance - Land and belongings that you give to your children and grandchildren when you die

Chapter 9

1. Answers may vary.

2. The people rejoice.

3. The people mourn.

4. Able men who fear God, do not lie, and hate covetousness.

5. The Fourth Commandment.

6. We must have good leaders.

7. The government becomes corrupt.

8. He stopped to help him. He did not ask the government to take care of him.

9. Good leaders can look in the Bible for what is just and right.

The Three Spheres of Government Activity:

Appointing Pastors – Church

Feeding and Clothing Children – Family

Capturing Criminals – State

Supporting poor widows and orphans – Church

Disciplining children – Family

Sending missionaries to other countries to preach the Gospel – Church

Deciding if a teenager is old enough to hunt – Family

Defending us from terrorists – State

Deciding which school children should attend – Family

Baptizing people – Church

Collecting tithes and offerings and spending that money – Church

Defending our borders from invasion – State

Prosecuting criminals and collecting taxes – State

Taking care of grandparents when they need care – Family

Vocabulary

Competent – Able to perform a task

Characteristic – A feature or quality belonging typically to a person, place, or thing and serving to identify it.
Standards – A required level of morality or quality
Justice – What is right (according to God's law)
Motivated – Excited about doing something
Citizen – An inhabitant of a particular city or nation
Judicial – The part of a civil magistrate that decided if you've broken the law
Legislature – The part of a civil magistrate that makes laws
Privilege – A special right or advantage
Irresponsible – Not fulfilling your duties or responsibilities
Immoral – Breaking God's laws

Chapter 10

1. The legislation and the judges/politics
2. If a civil law agrees with God's law then it is a good law.
3. The most basic civil law is capital punishment for murder.
4. Genesis 9.
5. Defending oneself from harm intended by another person.
6. They should flee to a city of refuge.
7. Prisons deny the biblical requirement for restitution.
8. Answers may vary.
9. The thief should pay twice the value for the bicycle and return the bicycle. If the bicycle cannot be returned, then the thief must pay four times the amount of the value of the bicycle.
10. The criminal must work to pay off the debt.
11. Two to three witnesses.
12. The maximum amount a government should ever tax is 10%.
13. Jesus told his disciples to buy swords for self-defense.

Vocabulary

Dictator – A tyrant, a very harsh political ruler with too much power
Penalty – A punishment for a crime committed
Legal – In accordance with the law of the country or state
Illegal – Against the law of the country or state
Capital Punishment – When the state puts somebody to death
Forethought – Planning ahead of time what you will do
Malice – Evil intent and hatred in your heart
Restitution – Returning to the victim the things you have stolen
Abomination – Something very horrible or appalling
Foreign Policy – How we get along with foreign countries
Abortion – Killing children in their mother's womb
Euthanasia – Killing the older people in our society